Business School

en
University

Unit 3
Costing and accounting systems

Written by Jonathan Winship and Martin Upton

Module Team

Dr Mike Lucas, *B292 Chair & Author*

Professor Jane Frecknall-Hughes, *Professional Certificate in Accounting Chair & Author*

Elizabeth R Porter, *Regional Manager & Author*

Jonathan Winship, *Author*

Stuart Munro, *Author*

Dr Vira Krakhmal, *Author*

Dr Pauline Gleadle, *Author*

Dr Jane Hughes, *Contributor*

Sam Cooper, *Programme Coordinator*

Emir Forken, *Programme Manager*

Dr Lesley Messer, *Head of Curriculum Operations*

Funmi Mapelujo, *Qualifications Manager*

Kelly Dobbs, *Curriculum Assistant*

External Assessor

Professor Stuart Turley, Manchester Business School

Critical Readers

Richard Davies

Dr Jane Hughes

Developmental Testers

Dr Teodora Burnand

Sam Cooper

Diane Jamieson

Sue Winship

Nicole Wright

Production Team

Simon Ashby, *Media Developer*

Martin Brazier, *Media Developer*

Anne Brown, *Media Assistant*

Vicky Eves, *Media Developer*

Diane Hopwood, *Rights Assistant*

Lee Johnson, *Media Project Manager*

Siggy Martin, *Print Buyer*

Kelvin Street, *Library*

Keith Wakeman, *Service Administrator*

The Module Team wishes to acknowledge use of some material from B680 *The Certificate in Accounting*.

This publication forms part of the Open University module B292 *Management accounting*. Details of this and other Open University modules can be obtained from the Student Registration and Enquiry Service, The Open University, PO Box 197, Milton Keynes MK7 6BJ, United Kingdom (tel. +44 (0)845 300 60 90; email general-enquiries@open.ac.uk).

Alternatively, you may visit the Open University website at www.open.ac.uk where you can learn more about the wide range of modules offered at all levels by The Open University.

To purchase a selection of Open University materials visit www.ouw.co.uk, or contact Open University Worldwide, Walton Hall, Milton Keynes MK7 6AA, United Kingdom for a brochure (tel. +44 (0)1908 858793; fax +44 (0)1908 858787; email ouw-customer-services@open.ac.uk).

The Open University

Walton Hall

Milton Keynes

MK7 6AA

First published 2011. Second edition 2012.

Edited and designed by The Open University.

Typeset in India by OKS Prepress Services, Chennai.

Printed in the United Kingdom by Cambrian Printers, Aberystwyth.

ISBN 978 1780 0 7382 8

2.1

FSC

Mixed Sources

Product group from well-managed forests and other controlled sources

Cert no. TT-COC-2200
www.fsc.org
© 1996 Forest Stewardship Council

Contents

Introduction

Unit 3 builds on your knowledge of the purpose and role of management accounting gained in Unit 1 and your knowledge of cost analysis gained in Unit 2. In this unit you will learn how inventory is accounted for and managed within the organisation, and the methods for calculating the cost of different types of products, processes and services. Accurate cost determination in an organisation is crucial for effective financial planning and control, which will be covered in the next unit, Unit 4.

Learning aims and outcomes of Unit 3

Upon completion of Unit 3, you are expected to be able to understand and explain the costing and accounting methods and systems which provide the management of an organisation with relevant and reliable information on which to base decisions. In particular, you should be able to:

1 understand the importance of accounting for inventory from both a financial accounting and a management accounting perspective

2 make recommendations to an organisation about improvements to its inventory management

3 explain the just-in-time approach to inventory management

4 understand integrated accounting systems combining both financial and cost accounts in one system of ledger accounts

5 calculate costs using the job costing and contract costing methods of costing

6 calculate the cost of a product or service from basic information using batch costing and process costing

7 understand and explain the difference between activity based costing and the more traditional approaches to costing units of production, service or market segments.

Note that no timings are specified for activities in this unit. In general, you should spend no longer than 20–25 minutes maximum on activities, though many will require a much shorter time than this.

SESSION 1 Inventory control

Introduction

Upon completion of Session 1 you are expected to be able to:

- understand the constituents of inventory costs
- calculate the economic order quantity (EOQ) for an organisation
- understand the effect of discounts on EOQ decisions
- calculate reorder levels and minimum and maximum levels of inventory
- explain what is meant by just-in-time inventory control and how it differs from traditional approaches.

In Session 1, you will learn about the costs of inventory, the nature of inventory control and quantitative methods for managing inventory. Investment in inventories represents a major asset for most organisations, and it is essential that inventories are managed efficiently so that such investments do not become unnecessarily large. An organisation should determine its optimum level of investment in inventories. To do this, two requirements must be met. First, the organisation must ensure that inventories are sufficient to meet the requirements of production and sales. Second, it should try to minimise the holding of surplus inventories and the cost of inventory holding. There is a constant trade-off between the costs and benefits of holding inventory.

1.1 Why hold inventories?

The only inventory held by wholesalers and retailers are goods for resale. Manufacturers, however, hold the following types of inventory.

1 **Direct material** – direct materials in inventory, awaiting use in the manufacturing process.
2 **Work-in-progress** – goods partly worked on, but not yet fully completed.
3 **Finished goods** – goods fully completed, but not yet sold.

As you learned in Unit 1, financial accounting is different from management accounting in that it is subject to external regulations which include accounting standards. One such standard requires that all inventory, whether it is direct material, work-in-progress or finished goods, be valued at cost or net realisable value (whichever is lower) and be presented as such in the published income statement and the published balance sheet. The **net realisable value** of inventory is the expected selling price, less any costs still to be incurred in selling it. For example, if a shoe maker sells shoes for £60 and estimates that each sale costs £3 in selling and distribution costs, the net realisable value for a pair of shoes is equal to £57.

Cost, as defined in this accounting standard, is all the expenditure incurred in getting a product or service to its present location and condition. This expenditure includes all related production overheads. Inventory must therefore be valued, for financial accounting purposes, using the absorption costing method you learned about in Unit 2.

The inventory records should contain an up to date record of inventories, both in terms of number of units and value. These records enable control of the inventories and also allow the value of inventories at any point in time to be ascertained. This involves recording the opening inventories at the beginning of a period, the receipt of new inventories and the return of goods to suppliers, along with the issue and return of inventories to and from production. The costing section of the accounts department is normally responsible for costing materials used in production.

The way in which inventory costs are charged to production can have a profound effect on the determination of the cost of production. It is important to recognise that there may be more than one way of measuring costs. Prices of bought in materials and components often vary over time, hence it is necessary to make an assumption about which particular units of material are being used, as different units may well have cost different amounts. There is a range of different methods of valuing inventories, each of which seeks to arrive at a value that approximates to the 'real' cost of the goods or raw materials used in production or sold or held in inventories, including:

- FIFO (first in, first out)
- LIFO (last in, first out)
- average cost
- standard cost
- market price.

FIFO is based on charging inventories used at the earliest purchase price. It assumes that an organisation uses the items purchased earliest first and that the items remaining in inventory are those purchased last. This may, or may not, correspond to the actual physical pattern of inventory usage. Using this method, the remaining inventory is valued at the most recent prices, which can be argued as being realistic. This method of inventory valuation is generally accepted by the tax authorities in the UK (it is the one recommended by Statement of Standard Accounting Practice (SSAP) No. 9, Stocks and Long-Term Contracts) and International Accounting Standard 2 Inventories (IAS 2), and is the normal basis for valuing inventories in published financial statements.

LIFO charges inventories to production at the most recent cost. In times of inflation it can be argued as being realistic, but it does mean that the remaining inventories tend to be undervalued in relation to current market prices. This method is not recommended as the basis for inventories' valuation in published financial statements.

Average cost is based on a calculation (i.e., total inventory cost/ total number of units of inventory) each time goods are issued to production. It is normally based on a weighted average calculation. Assuming that materials are bought at different prices, the average cost will not represent actual cost, but it can be argued that, from a cost comparison perspective, it provides a means for evening out fluctuations in buying prices.

In **standard costing**, a pre-determined cost is established for each item for a period and is then used for charging costs to products or services. It has the advantage of simplicity, although the charge may well differ from actual cost. Therefore, it is important to check the actual costs for a period against the standard cost and to ensure that differences (**variances**) are investigated and reflected in revised standard costs for the next period.

Market price is used when there is price volatility in the basic material cost because of market conditions. An example of a trade affected by this is the jewellery business, where the price of precious metals and stones fluctuates because of variations in supply and demand.

'Well it's inventory time again – you do the rocks and I'll do the sticks.'

Accounting for inventory, however, is not only important to enable an organisation to prepare published financial statements in accordance with its statutory obligations. The organisation needs to measure and manage inventories efficiently and effectively in order to generate the maximum possible financial return from the inventory. In this section, we will look at why organisations need to hold the right type of inventory as well as the right amount of such inventory in order to achieve this.

There are three main reasons for holding inventories:

1   The *transactions motive* occurs when there is a need to maintain inventories to meet production and sales needs, and it is not possible to meet these needs instantly.
2   An organisation might maintain additional inventories to meet unforeseen circumstances, for example, under-estimated future production and sales requirements. This *precautionary motive* applies to uncertain future demand.
3   An organisation might also use a *speculative motive* and maintain maximum or minimum levels of inventories to benefit from the expected increase or decrease in future prices.

Management should ascertain the optimum inventory level, which depends on a comparison of future cost savings from purchasing now and the increased cost resulting from holding additional inventory.

Where an organisation is able to predict accurately the demand for its inputs and outputs and it is confident that the prices of inputs will remain constant, it will have to consider only the transactions motive for holding inventories. In addition, an organisation will normally seek to minimise the amount of inventories held. This is because there are significant costs associated with holding inventories, as indicated below, such as:

- storage and handling costs
- financing costs (e.g., the interest on a bank overdraft used to finance purchase of inventory)
- the costs of pilferage (theft) and obsolescence
- the opportunity cost of tying up funds in this form of asset.

Inventory holding costs are usually estimated as a percentage of the inventory value and include estimated costs of financing, warehousing, insurance, obsolescence and shrinkage. Additionally, an organisation must recognise that, if the level of inventories held is too low, there will also be associated costs.

Activity 1.1 ....

What costs might a business incur as a result of holding too low a level of inventories? Try to write down at least three types of cost.

Feedback ....

You may have thought of some of the following costs:

- loss of sales, from being unable to provide the goods required immediately
- loss of goodwill from customers, from being unable to satisfy customer demand
- high transport costs incurred to ensure that inventories are replenished quickly
- lost production due to shortage of raw materials
- inefficient production scheduling due to shortages of raw materials
- purchasing inventories at a higher price than might otherwise have been possible in order to replenish inventories quickly.

1.2 The economic order quantity model

Buying small, frequent quantities lowers the average level of inventory and the associated costs of inventory holding, but increases the following ordering costs as more orders must be placed with suppliers:

- order processing and administrative costs
- handling and transportation costs.

Buying infrequently, large quantities of inventory lowers the overall ordering costs but increases the average level of inventory, resulting in higher inventory holding costs. The quantity that best reconciles these opposing tendencies is known as the **economic order quantity (EOQ)**. The EOQ is the order quantity that yields the lowest total costs of ordering and holding the inventory.

In its simplest form, the EOQ model assumes that demand is constant, so that inventories will be depleted evenly over time, and replenished instantly or within a constant lead time when they are needed. These assumptions lead to a 'saw tooth' pattern representing inventory movements, as shown in Figure 1.

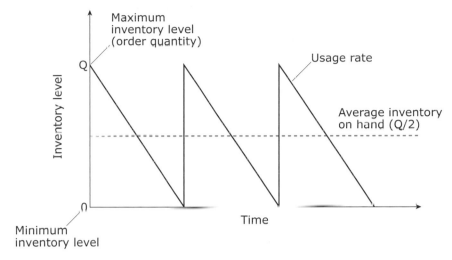

Figure 1   Patterns of inventory movement over time

It is assumed that there is a constant rate of usage of the inventory item, and that inventories are reduced to zero just as new inventories arrive. At time 0 there is a full level of inventory. This is steadily used as time passes. Just as it falls to zero, it is replaced. This pattern is then repeated. A constant order quantity is also assumed, equal to maximum inventory.

The EOQ model assumes that the only costs associated with inventory management are the costs of holding and the cost of ordering inventories. The model can be used to calculate the optimum size of a purchase order by taking account of both these costs. The cost of holding inventories can be substantial, and so management may try to minimise the average amount of inventories held. However, by reducing the level of inventories held, and therefore the holding costs, there will be a need to increase the number of orders during the period, and so ordering costs will rise.

It can be shown mathematically that the EOQ can be found by applying a formula that incorporates the basic relationships between holding and ordering costs and order quantities. These relationships can be stated as follows.

$$EOQ = \sqrt{\frac{2DC}{H}}$$

Where:

    D   represents the annual demand for the inventory item (expressed in units of the inventory item)

    C   represents the cost of placing an order

    H   represents the cost of holding one unit of inventory for one year

The EOQ mathematical formula presented above can also be presented graphically. Figure 2 shows how, as the level of inventory and the size of inventory orders increase, the annual costs of placing orders will decrease because fewer orders will be placed. However, the cost of holding inventory will increase, as there will be higher average inventory levels. The total cost curve, which is based on the sum of both holding costs and ordering costs, will fall until the point

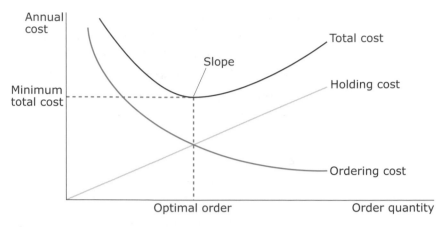

Figure 2   Economic order quantity graph

of optimal order quantity, which represents the minimum total cost. Thereafter, total costs begin to rise. The EOQ model seeks to identify the point of optimal order quantity at which total costs are minimised.

Small levels of inventory imply frequent reordering and high annual ordering costs against relatively low inventory holding costs. High levels of inventory imply exactly the opposite. There is, in theory, an optimum order size that will lead to the sum of ordering and holding costs (total costs) being at a minimum.

Activity 1.2 ....

ABC Ltd sells 2,000 items of a particular type of light switch in a year. It has been estimated that the cost of holding one light switch for a year is £4. The cost of placing an order for new inventory is estimated at £250. Calculate the EOQ for the light switch using the EOQ model and draw the EOQ graph.

Feedback ....

Your answer to this activity should be as follows:

$$EOQ = \sqrt{\frac{2 \times 2,000 \ items \times £250}{£4}} = 500 \ items$$

This will mean that the business will have to order light switches four times each year so that sales demand can be met (i.e., 2,000/500 = 4 times a year).

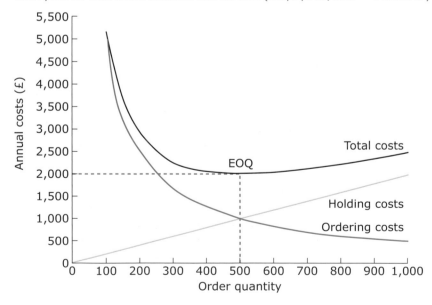

Figure 3   Economic order quantity graph

The order quantity obtained by using the EOQ should be interpreted with care, since the model is based on a number of limiting assumptions. In particular, it assumes that:

- demand for the product can be predicted with accuracy
- demand is constant over the period and does not fluctuate through seasonality or other reasons
- there is a constant reorder lead time
- no **safety inventory** is required (see Section 1.4)
- there are no discounts for bulk purchasing.

Another assumption that is made in calculating the total holding cost is that the average balance in inventory is equal to one half of the order quantity and follows from the assumption of constant demand. If a constant amount of inventory is not used per day, this assumption will be invalid. There is a distinct possibility that seasonal and cyclical factors will produce an uneven usage over time. It was also assumed that if a safety inventory were maintained, it would remain the same irrespective of the order size, and it could therefore be ignored in the calculation of average inventory. However, the size of safety inventory is probably not independent of order quantity, since relatively larger safety inventory is likely to be associated with smaller order quantities.

Despite a number of simplifying assumptions, the EOQ model can be developed to accommodate the problems of each of these limiting assumptions. Many businesses use this model (or a development of it) to help in the management of inventories.

1.3 Effect of discounts

Organisations often are able to obtain quantity discounts for larger purchase orders. Quite often the price paid per unit will not be the same for different order sizes, hence the purchase price per order must be taken into account when the economic order quantity is determined. Nevertheless, the basic EOQ formula can still be used to determine the optimum quantity to order. Buying in larger batches to take advantage of quantity discounts can lead to the following savings:

- a reduction in the ordering cost because a smaller number of orders is placed so as to benefit from the discounts
- a saving in purchase price.

However, the cost savings must be compared with the increased holding cost resulting from higher inventory levels when larger quantities are purchased. To determine whether or not a discount is beneficial, the benefits should be compared with the additional holding costs.

Let us consider an example of a business that obtains raw materials from a supplier at a cost of £14 per unit. The total annual demand for the product is 18,000 units. The holding cost is £8 per unit and the ordering cost is £10 per order. A quantity discount of five per cent of the purchase price is obtainable for orders of 2,000 units. Should the company order in batches of 2,000 units and benefit from the quantity discount?

The initial step is to calculate the economic order quantity and then to consider whether the benefits exceed the costs if the business obtains larger quantities to get the discounts. The calculation is as follows.

$$EOQ = \sqrt{\frac{2 \times 18,000 \times £10}{£8}} = 212 \text{ units}$$

The savings available to the business if it purchases in batches of 2,000 units instead of batches of 212 units are as follows.

Saving in purchase price (five per cent of annual purchase cost of £252,000 = 18,000 × £14) = £12,600

Saving in order cost:

$$\frac{DC}{Q} - \frac{DC}{Q_d} = \frac{18,000 \times £10}{212} - \frac{18,000 \times £10}{2,000} = £759$$

Where:

    D   represents the annual demand for the inventory item (expressed in units of the inventory item)

    C   represents the cost of placing an order

    Q   represents EOQ

    Q_d represents the quantity ordered to obtain the discount

Therefore, the total savings = £12,600 + £759 = £13,359.

The additional holding cost, if the larger quantity is purchased, is calculated as follows.

$$\frac{(Q_d - Q)H}{2} = \frac{(2,000 - 212) \times £8}{2} = £7,152$$

Where:

Q_d represents the quantity ordered to obtain the discount

Q represents EOQ

H represents the cost of holding one unit of inventory for one year

The additional savings of £13,359 exceed the additional costs, and the business should consider the order quantity of 2,000 units. If more discounts are available, for example, by obtaining in batches of 3,000 units, a similar analysis can be applied to compare the savings from purchasing in batches of 3,000 units and in batches of 2,000 units. The savings should then be compared with the additional holding costs.

1.4 Reorder level

So far, we have been looking at the reorder quantity. Now we will briefly consider the *reorder level*. This is the level of inventory at which a new order should be placed.

The management of inventories in a business of any size requires a sound system of recording inventory movements. Periodic inventory checks may be required to ensure that the amount of physical inventories held is consistent with what is indicated by the inventory records.

There should also be procedures for the reordering of inventories. Authorisation for both the purchase and the issue of inventories to production should be confined to a few senior staff. This should prevent problems of duplication and lack of coordination. To determine the point at which inventory should be reordered, information will be required concerning the lead time (i.e., the time between the placing of an order and the receipt of the goods) and the likely level of demand.

'We need to upgrade our computer system like yesterday.'

To work out the right reorder level, you need some data about how demand and lead times vary. You can then calculate the effects of different reorder levels. When demand and lead times are constant, it is easy to calculate the reorder level. It is simply the demand expected during the lead time. For example, if usage is 100 units per day and it always takes five days for an order to be delivered, the reorder level should be 500 units, that is, when the inventory level falls to 500 units a new order should be placed.

Activity 1.3 ....

An electrical retailer holds an inventory of a particular type of light bulb. The annual demand for the light bulb is 10,400 units, and the lead time for orders is four weeks. Demand for the light bulb is steady throughout the year. At what level of inventory should the business reorder, assuming that it is confident of the information given above?

Feedback ....

The average weekly demand for the switch is 10,400/52 weeks = 200 units. During the time between ordering new switches and receiving them, the quantity sold will be 4×200 units = 800 units, so the business should reorder no later than when the level held reaches 800 units, in order to avoid running out of inventory.

The **maximum inventory level** is the level above which the inventory of any item should not normally rise. Maximum level can be calculated by using the following formula:

Maximum level = [Reorder level – (Minimum usage × Minimum reorder period)] + EOQ

The **minimum inventory level** is the level below which inventory should not be allowed to fall. There is a danger of disrupting production and losing sales if inventory falls below this minimum level. Minimum level can be calculated by using the following formula:

Minimum level = Reorder level – (Average or normal usage × Reorder period)

Activity 1.4 ....

Normal usage	200 units per day
Maximum usage	260 units per day
Minimum usage	140 units per day
Reorder period	50 to 60 days
Economic order quantity	10,000 units

Calculate reorder level and maximum and minimum inventory levels by using information provided above.

Feedback ....

Reorder level = Maximum usage × Maximum reorder period

$\qquad$ = 260×60

$\qquad$ = 15,600 units

Maximum level = [Reorder level – (Minimum usage × reorder period)] + EOQ

$\qquad$ = [15,600 – (140 × 50)] + 10,000 = 18,600 units

Minimum level = Reorder level – (Normal usage × Reorder period)

$\qquad$ = 15,600 – (200 × 55*) = 4,600 units

*(50 + 60)/2 = 55

Stock-out cost is the opportunity cost resulting from running out of inventory. For example, a shortage of finished goods inventories will result in a loss of revenue (and profit) if customer orders cannot be met on demand. When a stock-out occurs for raw materials and work-in-progress inventories, this is likely to result in disruptions to production and other inefficiencies. Evidently, stock-out costs are very difficult to quantify.

It is hard to predict the demand for inventories with certainty and there is also a degree of uncertainty linked to the delivery of the inventories. To minimise this uncertainty, a business will hold a level of safety inventory of raw materials, work-in-progress and finished goods. Consequently, safety inventories are the inventories that are held in excess of the expected demand during the delivery lead time to avoid running out of inventories.

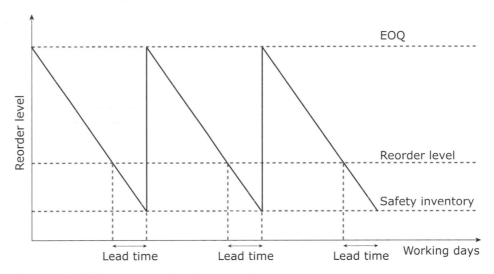

Figure 4 EOQ model and safety inventory

In Figure 4, the lead time plays an important role in the determination of the safety inventory. The acceptable level of inventory should be determined by considering whether the cost of holding safety inventory exceeds the costs that will be incurred if the company runs out of inventory.

The following text box explains how investments in the inventory create opportunity costs and increase the risk of cash flow shortage.

Raturi and Singhal, in their 1990 study '...show how an increase in lead time or ordering cost may lead to increased risk. Firms with large lead time or ordering cost should hence use a larger opportunity cost of capital to account for the increased risk of cash flows. ... More frequent ordering, if not accompanied by a simultaneous reduction in ordering cost, could lead to increased riskiness. Furthermore, within a firm, the opportunity cost of capital should be larger for product lines that have larger lead times, larger ordering costs or larger time between review and vice versa. This not only accounts for the higher riskiness of the cash flows, but also gives those departments incentives to reduce ordering cost, and review and control their inventory levels more frequently (and hence implement procedures and systems that reduce inventory levels), or reduce their lead time. Such efforts could also provide a number of other indirect benefits like improved product quality, more linear flow of production, etc.'

Source: Raturi, A.S. and Singhal V.R. (1990) 'Estimating the opportunity cost of capital for inventory investments', *OMEGA: The International Journal of Management Science*, vol. 18, no. 4, pp. 407–13

Activity 1.5

....

Assume the same facts as in Activity 1.3. However, we are also told that the business maintains a safety inventory of 300 units. At what level should the business reorder?

Feedback

....

The reorder point = the expected level of demand during the lead time + the level of safety inventory = 800 + 300 = 1,100 units.

1.5 Just-in-time inventory control

Just-in-time (JIT) inventory control refers to a system in which materials arrive exactly as they are needed in production. Demand drives production and immediate delivery eliminates waiting times and the need for inventories. The JIT system requires businesses to restructure their relationship with suppliers and place smaller and more frequent orders. Businesses moving towards JIT inventory argue that the full cost of holding inventories (including inventory storage space, spoilage and opportunity costs not recorded in the accounting system) have been dramatically under-estimated. At the same time, building partnerships with suppliers and using electronic systems for order related activities significantly reduce ordering costs.

The JIT inventory control model is an alternative to the EOQ model. As discussed earlier, the EOQ model is concerned with minimising the overall cost of inventory, having regard to ordering and holding costs. It is not concerned with minimising the amount of inventory held. The JIT approach, on the other hand, is concerned with minimising the amount of inventory and ideally eliminating inventory all together. The existence of inventory often conceals much waste and inefficiency. By removing inventory, the JIT approach also eliminates waste and inefficiency. Considerable savings in material handling expenses can also be made by requiring suppliers to inspect materials before their delivery and to guarantee their quality.

This improved service is obtained by giving more business to fewer suppliers (who can provide high quality and reliable deliveries) and placing long-term purchasing orders. Therefore, the supplier has assurance of long-term sales and can plan to meet his/her demand.

The JIT approach involves a continuous commitment to the pursuit of excellence in all phases of inventory control, with supplier and customer working in partnership to achieve this. However, if JIT is adopted and something goes wrong with the supplier or with the process of receiving supplies from the supplier, sales to customers and any production scheduled have to stop.

Activity 1.6 ....

List as many things as possible that could go wrong, causing a JIT system to fail.

Feedback ....

Your list may have included the following.

- The organisation's computer system may crash and fail to place an order with the supplier.
- The wrong order quantity may be given to the supplier.
- The wrong items may be ordered.
- The supplier's computer system may crash and fail to receive notification of an order being placed.
- The supplier may have insufficient inventory available.
- Failure to pay the supplier may result in sudden withdrawal of the JIT facility. (Consider what happens to any cheques you write if you become overdrawn at the bank!)
- There may be a road haulage strike or 'go-slow'.
- Chaos or traffic on the roads may result in deliveries from the supplier being held up in transit.
- The wrong delivery quantity may be sent by the supplier.
- The wrong items may be sent by the supplier.

All of the above would be less of a problem if traditional inventory control methods with safety inventories were in place rather than a JIT system because errors *could be* dealt with from inventories held.

Only when a customer wants to buy something not held in inventory would a traditional inventory control system be as susceptible to these errors and problems as a JIT one. In fact, because of the priority relationship between JIT suppliers and their customers, a traditional system is inferior to a JIT system when customers want to buy goods not held in inventory.

Organisations that have a JIT relationship with their suppliers claim the following benefits:

- lower holding costs (there will still be some costs incurred while the goods are being prepared for distribution to customers, unless the supplier has agreed to send orders direct to the ordering organisation's customers)
- greater production flexibility (provided that suppliers agree to respond rapidly to switches from previously 'normal' supply requests)
- better response to customers' requirements
- no possibility of obsolete inventory
- a closer relationship with suppliers
- more contented customers (as they receive the goods they want to buy in a more consistently timely manner).

In a production environment where JIT is applied to production scheduling, the basis of the JIT approach is that each process produces only what is required by the next stage or process in the production cycle. The demand for production comes directly from that next stage or process. If work is not progressing as planned and JIT production can not be delivered, the next stage or process can adjust its instructions to production. In this way, work-in-progress inventories are not allowed to build up.

If a disruption occurs in any one process, later stages or processes must stop producing (once their supplies run out) until the problem is resolved. Indeed, it is an essential part of this approach that it is everyone's responsibility to remedy a problem anywhere in the system so that the performance of the whole system can be improved. This 'demand-pull control' system is shown in Figure 5. Customer orders (dotted lines) drive production. The process starts with the customers who place demands on the production facilities, which in turn place demands on upstream processes throughout the system, thereby eliminating excess inventory.

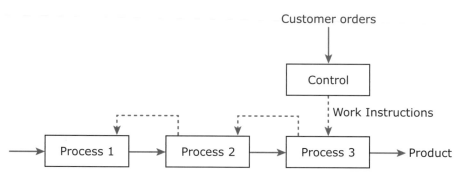

Figure 5   Demand-pull control

The demand-pull approach relies on cooperation within the system and by suppliers within the system. At all stages, there must be communication and cooperation between each stage or process to meet the input requirements for the next stage or process.

JIT has become increasingly popular in Western manufacturing companies as they seek to emulate the success of the Japanese motor car manufacturers (particularly Toyota) with which firms it originated. Modern technology has enabled some organisations, like Wal-Mart Stores and Dell, to achieve the JIT goal of almost zero inventory holding.

Activity 1.7 ....

From a supplier's point of view, what would be required from the purchaser to make it worthwhile to provide the level of service and quality demanded by JIT?

Feedback ....

Apart from a higher price (which, in any case, may not be achievable in a competitive market), a supplier would probably look for a long-term commitment to enable it to invest in the necessary systems (and, perhaps, equipment) for the contract. It would prefer simply to operate order systems with minimal paperwork, and a guarantee of regular prompt payment against daily, weekly or, possibly, monthly invoices. Clearly, a move to JIT implies a significant change in relationships with suppliers and, indeed, all purchasing practices.

As Table 1 shows, JIT has its costs as well as benefits.

Table 1 Costs and benefits of JIT

Benefits	Disadvantages
Lower holding costs	Disrupted production if inventories are not available
Greater production flexibility	Loss of bulk discounts
Better response to customer requirements	Potentially increased shipping costs; small order shipping
Elimination of non-value added activities. The latter are activities that add no real value to the product or service, making such activities or action a form of waste, for example, overtime premia, uneven scheduling of work, unnecessary meetings, down-time.	Need for additional facilities to cope with high demand
	Loss of ability to stockpile when prices are low
Minimisation of lead time involved in manufacturing and selling a product. It can consist of process time, inspection time, move time and storage time.	Potential inability to deal with exceptional demand
No obsolete inventory	
Better understanding of own processes	
Closer relationship with suppliers	

Summary

In this session, we have looked at inventory control. The objective of inventory control is to optimise the inventory holding levels. The costs of maintaining inventory include ordering costs and holding costs. Ordering costs decline and holding costs increase when the order quantity is increased. We looked at how to calculate the economic order quantity (EOQ) for an organisation when provided with appropriate input data, including potential discounts. The principles of the reorder level method of inventory control were also introduced.

When uncertainty of demand and lead times are incorporated into the analysis, businesses must hold safety inventory to cover the possibility that demand and lead time may be different from that assumed in the EOQ calculation, hence safety inventory should be determined.

This session also introduced you to just-in-time inventory control techniques that focus on reducing the cost of placing an order and reducing or eliminating inventory. For JIT to work well, the following conditions must apply:
- good management information systems
- a good relationship with local suppliers
- high quality production and supplies.

SESSION **2 Integrated accounting systems**

Introduction

Upon completion of Session 2, you are expected to be able to:

- understand the legal requirements governing cost accounting
- recognise the principles of double-entry bookkeeping
- understand how management accounting is dependent upon the cost accounting system
- understand how a system of integrated accounts combines both financial and cost accounts in one system of accounts
- prepare a simple set of integrated cost and financial accounts
- understand the advantages of an integrated system of accounts.

The task of the manager is to plan, communicate, motivate, organise and control the part of the organisation that is his/her responsibility. These activities are undertaken under conditions of uncertainty, but the difficulties are eased if management information systems deliver reliable information concerning what is actually happening. The management information systems must provide the right information to the right person at the right time, in the right form and at an acceptable cost. The system on which we will concentrate our attention is a bookkeeping system that contains both financial and cost accounts. This is termed an **integrated accounting system**.

2.1 Integrated accounting systems

At the beginning of this unit, we learned that it is a legal requirement for the inventory recorded in the published financial statements to be determined using absorption costing not marginal costing (as you may also recall from Unit 2). All accounting systems in a manufacturing business, however small, must thus ensure that the measurement of any work-in-progress and finished goods must include all related production overheads, as well as the direct costs.

A further legal requirement that affects all organisations, not just manufacturing ones, is that all costs incurred in a financial period should be accurately recorded and summarised in the income statement, along with all income earned in the same period, in order to determine the profit/loss (or surplus/deficit) for that period. The costs incurred in a period include costs that have been invoiced at the period end as well as costs that have only been accrued, that is, costs such as electricity which may not have been invoiced but which still have to be recorded in the financial records, even if based on an estimate.

Every organisation is legally obliged to keep records of all costs that are incurred in a financial period, including details of whether these costs have been paid for or not by the end of the financial period. This detailed recording of costs in a financial period is made possible by a system of financial record keeping known as the **double-entry bookkeeping system**.

The double-entry bookkeeping system is a logical, integrated system of keeping financial records or accounts in a financial accounting system. It does this by ensuring that each individual transaction is recorded in at least two different accounts, thus creating a double entry for every financial transaction. This system reflects the two sides of the transactions, for example, gaining an asset but also creating a liability when raw material inventory is purchased on credit.

A detailed explanation of the double-entry system and how it underpins the financial statements in a financial accounting system is beyond the scope of this module. On the B292 website, however, there is a link to material from B190 (*Introduction to bookkeeping and accounting*) which is designed to teach students this topic. You are strongly recommended to work through this material if you have not completed B190 or B291 (*Financial accounting*).

A **financial accounting system** is intended to inform management how much is owed to and by various external parties and to monitor overall performance of the organisation. It has instrumental as well as legal purposes. Such a system is designed to record and summarise all transactions affecting income accounts, expense accounts, asset accounts, liability accounts and capital accounts. A **cost accounting** system, on the other hand, is set up to enable an organisation to work out the cost of products or services sold, or the cost of particular jobs, contracts or manufacturing processes. There is no legal requirement to produce this information.

CIMA Official Terminology, p. 3, defines integrated accounts as 'a set of accounting records that integrates both financial and cost accounts using a common input of data for all accounting purposes'.

Management depends on an effective cost accounting system for planning, control and decision making purposes. Good information is needed, for instance, about the cost of each product or service that is sold by the organisation. The cost accounting system provides such information, drawing on data from the financial accounts and other records such as cost cards and time sheets. The management accountant then interprets this information, as well as other relevant information, such as economic forecasts and sales figures, and prepares reports for the use of the managers of the organisation. As you learned in Unit 1, these reports are tailored, as appropriate, to the strategic, tactical and operational level at which managers are operating.

2.2 Designing and operating integrated accounting systems

It makes sense to use a common source of data for all accounting purposes, whether to meet legal requirements or to aid decision making. This is much cheaper, quicker and more reliable than using separate sources of data for financial accounting on the one hand, and management accounting on the other.

Fortunately, modern computer technology allows even small businesses to design and operate integrated systems of accounts which combine both financial and cost accounts in one system.

The following case study should help you to understand how the same source data can be analysed and presented in different ways for different purposes.

Let's Build is a small sole tradership owned by a self-employed builder, Pat Kemal, who uses hourly paid labourers to help him on different construction jobs. Pat also employs a part time clerk to help him with the administration of his business.

In the course of a financial year the organisation needs to keep a number of financial accounts in order to record and report its costs for the year. (Pat does not use credit in his business, so his accounts are relatively simple.) During the same period, the business keeps accounts for each construction job, as Pat wishes to know the cost of each job, not just his overall costs as summarised in the income statement for the year.

Pat uses a simple computerised accounting package to record his source data (such as time sheets for direct labour and invoices for materials and consumables used). The program automatically posts these data to two corresponding financial accounts (as per the rules of double-entry bookkeeping) and updates the running balance on each account. Each account is linked in an integrated accounting system which allows reports such as an income statement, which collates all the cost and income accounts in one report, to be produced automatically.

This accounting package is also set up to record the cost accounts for each construction job. When the relevant cost data are recorded, the program automatically posts these data to an individual job account as well as to the relevant financial account by corresponding entry.

Pat has kept the following job sheet to record the costs of Job 7, the seventh completed construction job for Let's Build in his financial year.

	Job 7
	£
Materials used	8,143
Consumables used	975
Direct labour	2,140
Share of depreciation on equipment	972

It is important to recognise that before the costs above were allocated to Job 7 they were first recorded in his financial accounting system according to the rules of double-entry bookkeeping. All expenses, such as materials, consumables and direct labour, were paid for directly from the bank.

So, for example, the purchase of raw materials for £54,060 from suppliers is first recorded in the materials purchases account in the financial accounting system (see below). All materials that are bought are debited to this account and with a corresponding credit to the bank account, according to the rules of double-entry bookkeeping.

Then, as materials are consumed by each job, the material purchases account is credited (Cr) and the particular job cost account is debited (Dr) (see below).

Material purchases account

Dr		£	Cr		£
	Bank a/c	54,060		Jobs 1–6	43,850
				Job 7	8,143
				Balance c/d	2,067
		54,060			54,060
	Balance b/d	2,067			

The same principle applies to all the other expenses consumed by the earlier jobs (Jobs 1–6) and Job 7. Every expense incurred by the business is initially recorded in the debit side of the relevant financial expense account (materials, consumables, salaries and wages, and depreciation of equipment). Then, as we have done for the material purchases account, the expense account is credited and the relevant job cost account is debited as these expenses are charged to particular jobs.

A balance will arise on the material purchases account, which reflects that more materials were purchased than used on Jobs 1–7, hence leaving a debit balance. This is why on the opposite side to the 'Balance c/d' figure, a 'Balance b/d' figure is needed to represent a closing debit balance (which then becomes the opening balance for the next period). This means that the materials purchases account also acts as a materials inventory account, as the balance of £2,067 carried down should be capable of being verified by a physical inventory check or count.

At the end of the period, the Job 7 cost account will also be balanced, and the balance (which will be, effectively, the total of all costs transferred from the financial accounts) will be debited to Let's Build's cost of sales account.

Job 7 cost account

Dr	£	Cr	£
Material purchases a/c	8,143	Cost of sales	12,230
Consumables a/c	975		
Salaries and wages a/c	2,140		
Depreciation expense a/c	972		
	12,230		12,230

Below are the remaining expenses accounts after they have also been charged to Job 7.

The credit side of consumables, salaries and wages, and depreciation of equipment will reflect the transfer of expenditure relevant to Job 7, with corresponding debit transaction to the Job 7 cost account. The balances are usually transferred to the income statement as end of period expenses. Those balances relating to balance sheet items will be reflected on the period end balance sheet, and will form opening balances on the relevant financial accounts for the next period.

Consumables

Dr	£	Cr	£
Bank	6,839	Jobs 1–6	5,850
		Job 7	975
		Transferred to income statement a/c	14
	6,839		6,839

Salaries and wages

Dr	£	Cr	£
Bank	19,585	Jobs 1–6	12,840
		Job 7	2,140
		Transferred to income statement a/c	4,605
	19,585		19,585

Depreciation of equipment

Dr	£	Cr	£
Depreciation expense	8,474	Jobs 1–6	5,832
		Job 7	972
		Transferred to income statement a/c	1,670
	8,474		8,474

At the end of the period, the cost of goods sold is transferred from the Jobs 1–6 and Job 7 cost accounts (credit side) to the cost of sales financial account (debit side), and from there to the income statement.

You will see in the cost of sales account below that Let's Build has debited costs separately for Jobs 1–6 carried out earlier in the financial year (easy to do as they have been completed). Job 7 turns out to be the last construction job for the financial period, in this case the financial period ended 31 December 20X5.

Cost of sales

Dr	£	Cr	£
Jobs 1–6	68,372	Transferred to income statement a/c	80,602
Job 7	12,230		
	80,602		80,602

Note that the balance on the material purchases account at the end of the year is £2,067. This balance is not part of the cost of sales figure for the year, that is, it does not represent an expense for the year. (The figure for cost of sales in the income statement includes only that purchased material that has been used up in completing Jobs 1–7 in the course of the year). The materials purchase balance of £2,067 is recorded as inventory in the current assets part of the balance sheet.

The double-entry bookkeeping system used by Pat records all expenses in his business, not just those related to specific jobs. As a result, the income statement will show expenses for rent, heating/lighting, etc., that are not chargeable to a specific job. This double-entry bookkeeping system also allows a periodic income statement and balance sheet to be produced as well as detailed reports to managers.

Income statement for Let's Build for the year ended 31st December 20X5

		£	£
Sales*			151,716
Less	Cost of sales: (£68,372 + £12,230)		(80,602)
Gross profit			71,114
Less	Expenses:		
	Rent	7,200	
	Heating/lighting	705	
	Insurance	1,620	
	Office expenses	745	
	Consumables	14	
	Salaries and wages	4,605	
	Depreciation	1,670	
			(16,559)
Net profit			54,555

*Sales and certain other cost figures are assumed here for the purposes of completing this illustration. They would be extracted from the accounting records that Let's Build maintains.

2.3 Advantages of using an integrated accounting system

The main advantage of integrated accounting systems is that such systems require only one set of accounting records. They thereby avoid the possible danger of having two sets of records with different figures.

The disadvantage of integrated accounting systems is that they are supposed to serve external reporting requirements and provide internal management information, which at times may be contradictory. For example, the valuation of inventories in an integrated accounting system must conform to statutory requirements, while management might prefer to use marginal costing to value closing inventories.

Computer software can now overcome these disadvantages and modern accounting systems are integrated systems, incorporating coding systems which allow basic data to be analysed and presented for different purposes, and which automatically update accounts as well as track customer, supplier, product and job information. In addition, the software permits the user to produce and print a number of reports, of which the cost of a particular job, the income statement and the balance sheet are just three. Additionally, computerised integrated accounting systems have the following advantages.

Accuracy – there is less chance of error as only one entry is required for each of the source data.

Speed – data entry is quicker because input screens are automatically linked to databases of all the computerised records, including customer, supplier and inventory records.

Volume – large volumes of data can be handled and processed easily.

Automated documentation – invoices, statements, cheques and VAT statements, etc., are all automated.

Updated information – the accounting records are automatically updated so all account balances, both cost and financial, are up to date.

Availability of information – data are instantly available to different users at different locations at the same time.

Management information – a number of reports can be produced to improve management of the business.

Presentation of information – financial information can be produced in graphical format.

Cost savings – accounting packages reduce time spent doing accounts and keeping records.

Ease of use – accounting packages can be used by non-specialists.

Accountability – a full **audit trail**, referenced to original documentation, should satisfy the needs of **auditors** and regulators.

Summary

Having studied this session you should now be able to explain the principles of the integration of the cost accounts with the financial accounting system. You should also be able to prepare a simple set of integrated accounts, given opening balances and appropriate transaction information.

The integrated accounting system merges cost and financial accounting to form one inseparable accounting function. It reduces the amount of work required in cost accounting by preventing duplication in processing and recording business transactions.

SESSION **3 Job, batch and contract costing**

Introduction

Upon completion of Session 3 you are expected to be able to:

- explain the differences between job, batch and contract costing
- describe how to calculate costs under job, batch and contract costing
- explain the problems associated with determining costs per job, batch and contract
- explain how profit can be calculated and recognised on unfinished contracts.

In this session, you will learn about three of four different approaches to costing – job, batch and contract costing – and about the practical issues that have to be addressed when adopting them. The fourth approach – process costing – is covered in Session 4 of this unit.

All organisations need to ascertain the costs of activities taking place and decide on appropriate methods of achieving cost control. Costing is not an exact science. It requires judgement and, indeed, common sense, in recognising management's need for information and weighing this against the cost of collecting such information.

You might think that we would need 100 per cent accuracy in the information but, if this costs ten times as much as it would do to achieve 99 per cent accuracy, management has to decide whether the additional expenditure is justified. This must be coupled with the recognition that, in any event, some of the costs allocated to a unit of output may be based on subjective judgement. This is particularly the case with the absorption of indirect costs into a product or service.

In this session, we will consider specific costing methods and how they are applied in practice. The various methods of costing described in this session relate to commercial businesses. However, the underlying principles are equally applicable to public sector and not-for-profit organisations.

The methods described in this session tend to use absorption costing as the basic approach, but you should now understand that marginal costing concepts could be useful where decisions affecting changes in volume are needed.

3.1 Job costing

Job costing is used in businesses that perform work on specific jobs or orders. A job cost system identifies the costs incurred which are then allocated or apportioned to the job. The job cost system shows (see Figure 6) the costs of materials, labour and overheads incurred by a particular job.

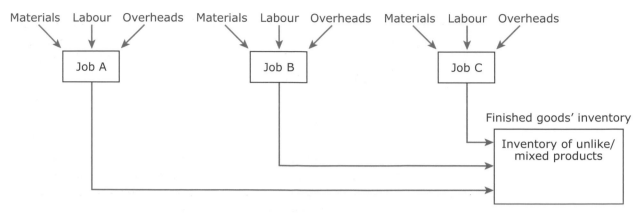

Figure 6   Job costing

Table 2 shows details of a job cost record which includes direct materials, direct labour and other direct costs to give the prime cost of production. The addition of indirect costs (production overhead) gives the total production cost of a job.

Table 2   Illustration of a job cost record

Customer reference – AB3		Product Code - 5997
Production description	Quantity	£
Direct materials:		
Type A	kg	10,000
Type B	kg	10,000
Type C	litres	10,000
Direct labour:		
Employee A	hrs	1,600
Employee B	hrs	1,600
Employee C	hrs	1,600
Prime cost of production		34,800
Indirect materials		2,700
Indirect labour		2,700
Other indirect costs		2,700
Total production overhead		8,100
Total job cost		42,900

The costs of direct materials should be recorded as the materials are used. Material costs for each job are determined from **material requisition notes** (stores requisitions). Materials are specifically obtained for the job and need to be priced by the purchasing department. Each requisition will have a job number and that number will be entered in the record so that the materials can be charged to the right job cost record.

Direct labour will be calculated using hours worked and the hourly rate for each employee. The hours worked will be collected from employee time sheets which show each job under its own number.

Other direct costs will be charged to jobs by entering the appropriate job number on the expense invoice.

Job costing requires the maintenance of adequate production records. Each job must be given its individual works order number and the separate orders must be easily identifiable at all stages of production.

The full cost of any particular job is the sum of those costs that can be measured specifically in respect of the job (direct costs) and a share of those costs that create the environment in which production (of an object or service) can take place, but which cannot easily be traced to a particular job (overheads).

The main purpose of job costing is to determine the profit or loss made on each job and to be able to show the cost to date of inventories of work-in-progress at the end of an accounting period.

Job costing is used for activities where the business's output consists of a series of separate jobs, all of which have a different mix of cost elements, such as materials, labour and indirect costs. Examples might include building repairs, construction and car servicing. Other examples include work done for clients by professionals, such as accountants, consultants and solicitors.

The basic approach is to ensure that an accounting system is in operation that enables the costs to be captured and then allocated or apportioned to the appropriate job. This includes materials used, direct labour incurred on the job and the apportionment of indirect costs. It follows that, for a job costing system to work effectively, there must be a comprehensive system of recording materials, labour and indirect costs.

> The accounting system must enable costs to be determined and appropriately attributed to each particular job.

Inventory records must be designed so that all materials used on a particular job are charged to it. These materials may be issued from inventory or specifically ordered for the job. Labour records need to ensure that a worker's time is accurately recorded and allocated to the relevant job cost records. This is normally done with time sheets that record how much of an employee's time should be allocated to the job (or jobs) on which the worker has been engaged.

Production overhead costs will be shared among the jobs to which they relate. As we have seen, the indirect costs are more complex and involve the subjective assessment of an appropriate method established by management for assigning indirect costs to jobs. To illustrate this, we shall use the number of direct labour hours as the means of assigning indirect costs. This method is the most frequently used approach for job costing.

To allocate indirect costs, we need to take a forward view of the number of productive labour hours in a future period and the budgeted level of indirect costs. Assume that the budgeted level of indirect costs is £14,000 and the planned number of productive hours is 1,600. The planned indirect cost per direct labour hour is £8.75, which is calculated as follows:

$$\frac{£14,000}{1,600} = £8.75 \text{ per direct labour hour}$$

An argument in favour of charging indirect costs based on the number of direct labour hours is that it seeks to link costs which are essentially time related, as labour is normally paid on a time basis. A problem might arise when the total number of direct labour hours chargeable is different from that envisaged at the start of the period. This will obviously lead to an under- or over-recovery of indirect costs (as discussed in Session 4 of Unit 2). For example, if only 1,500 hours were worked in the period against a plan of 1,600 hours, there would be £875 (100 × £8.75) under-recovered, which represents an additional £875 that must be shared out among the cost of all the jobs undertaken. The result is that profits for the jobs undertaken will be £875 less in total than anticipated.

If the number of chargeable hours worked was 1,660, there would have been an over-recovery of indirect costs of £525 (60 × £8.75). This means that £525 too much has been added to the costs of the jobs undertaken, so profit for these jobs will have been understated by £525. The more accurate the assessment of future levels of activity, the more accurate the job costs. The more accurate the job costs, the more effective are the planning decisions (e.g., pricing) that can be made based on those job costs.

It is also important to note that whether a cost is direct or indirect depends on the item being costed. Consider the following activity as an example of the cost object.

Activity 3.1 ....

Sparkles Ltd is a business that employs electricians to undertake a variety of work for its domestic customers, from replacing fuses to installing complete wiring systems in houses.

In respect of a particular job done by Sparkles Ltd, into which category (direct or indirect) would each of the following costs fall?

- Rent of the premises where Sparkles Ltd stores its inventories of cable and other materials.
- The wages of the electricians who did the job.
- The salary of Sparkles Ltd's accountant.
- Depreciation of the tools used by the electricians.
- The cost of cable and other materials used on the job.

Feedback ....

Only the electrician's wages spent on the particular job and the cost of the cable and other materials used on the job are direct costs. It is possible to measure how much time (and therefore the labour cost) was spent on the particular job and the amount of materials used on the job.

All of the other costs are general costs of running the business and, as such, must form part of the full cost of doing the job, but they cannot be directly measured in respect of the particular job.

Now, let us look at another of the approaches to costing. This time we shall focus on the special form called **batch costing**.

3.2 **Batch costing**

Batch costing is used where a number of identical items is produced at the same time.

Batch costing is a modification of job costing but, rather than dealing with one specific order for a customer (for which job costing would be used), it deals with situations where similar or identical items are manufactured in batches. Batch production is widely used in manufacturing processes in such industries as car manufacturing, shoe production or assembling products for the building industry, such as windows. In the motor industry, batches involve making several vehicles with a particular specification, such as electrically operated sun-roofs. The shoe industry is concerned with particular styles, colours and sizes and similar considerations apply in the manufacture of windows.

Activity 3.2

List four industries, other than those named above, which you think might use batch costing methods and name the unit of cost in each case.

(a)

(b)

(c)

(d)

Feedback

Four other industries and their unit of cost might be as follows:

(a) domestic appliance manufacturing – the units of each line of product (e.g., refrigerator, cooker, washing machine) are produced by the batch
(b) toy manufacturing – units of each type of toy are produced by the batch (e.g., dolls, games)
(c) garments – units of each style of garment are produced by the batch
(d) furniture – units of each product are produced by the batch (e.g., tables, chairs, desks, beds, wardrobes).

Note that special one-off jobs, such as a custom-designed suit or a custom-sized bed, would be costed using job costing, not batch costing.

As with other costing approaches, direct labour, materials and expenses are charged to the batch. To this is added an appropriate proportion of the indirect costs applied normally on absorption costing principles. In capital-intensive industries, this might well embrace **activity based costing (ABC)** concepts. (We shall look at activity based costing in Session 5 of this unit.)

A cost issue frequently associated with batch costing is set-up costs incurred as the production equipment is adjusted to meet the requirements of a new batch. These are direct costs of a fixed character for each batch and, clearly, the greater the number of units produced, the lower the cost of each unit will be. There is a balance to be struck between the batch size and the economic quantities required during a particular time. (You do not want to make more than you want or less than you need, or costs become higher than they should for each item made.)

Activity 3.3   ....

A company manufactures to order gadgets for mobile phones. The direct costs of producing an order for 100 gadgets (Batch XYZ) in a particular period are as follows.

Direct materials	£6,000
Direct labour	50 hours manufacturing at £5 per hour; 100 hours assembling at £4 per hour
Direct expenses	£200

The total indirect costs (and associated labour hours) for the production lines for the period are as follows.

Overheads		
Manufacturing	£3,000	250 labour hours
Assembling	£5,000	500 labour hours
Selling and administrative costs	10 per cent of factory cost	

Calculate the cost per unit for Batch XYZ.

Feedback   ....

The first step is to calculate the overhead absorption rate for the production departments:

$$\text{Manufacturing} = \frac{£3,000}{250 \text{ hours}} = £12 \text{ per labour hour}$$

$$\text{Assembling} = \frac{£5,000}{500 \text{ hours}} = £10 \text{ per labour hour}$$

Batch XYZ	**£**	**£**
Direct material		6,000
Direct labour	50 hours × £5	250
	100 hours × £4	400
Direct expenses		200
Total direct cost		6,850
Overheads	50 hours × £12	600
	100 hours × £10	1,000
Factory cost		8,450
Selling and administrative cost (10 per cent of factory cost)		845
Total cost		9,295

$$\text{Cost per unit} = = \frac{£9,295}{100 \text{ gadgets}} = £92.95$$

3.3 Contract costing

Contract costing is job costing on a large scale that incorporates estimates of revenue and profit. Contract costing is used in businesses that have major long-term contracts, such as civil engineering or shipbuilding. The main features of contract costing are:

- a formal contract is made between customer and supplier
- work is undertaken to a customer's special requirements

- the work is for a relatively long duration, that is, lasting a number of financial periods
- the work is frequently constructional in nature
- the method of costing is similar to job costing
- the work is frequently based on a particular site.

Job costing is appropriate where numerous individual jobs are likely to be completed during the course of a year. Contract costing is appropriate if only a few major contracts will be undertaken, and over a period typically longer than one year. Given that organisations will have a relatively small number of contracts in a year, charging costs to a contract is relatively easy and all direct costs are allocated to individual contract accounts. These costs might well include what might be regarded as indirect costs, such as managerial expenses, using other methods of costing, because they can be specifically identified with a particular contract.

Contract costing is job costing on a large scale that incorporates estimates of revenue and profit.

Given the length of time over which contracts may extend, the calculation of work-in-progress at the financial year end and the extent to which profit is recognised as the contract progresses pose particular problems. Both these matters are related, as the value of work-in-progress determines the annual profit of each contract.

The potential issues in contract costing relate to the following.

- *Identifying direct costs.* Because of the large size of the job, many cost items which are usually thought of as production overheads are charged as direct costs of the contract (e.g., supervision, hire of plant, depreciation and so on).
- *Low indirect costs.* Many costs normally classed as overheads are charged as direct costs of a contract.
- *Difficulties of cost control.* Because of the size of some contracts and some sites, there are often cost control problems (materials usage and losses, pilferage, labour supervision, damage to and loss of plant and tools).
- *Dividing the profit between different accounting periods.* When a contract covers more than one accounting period, how should the profit (or loss) on the contract be divided between the periods?

Let us consider the following example using the budgeted costs on a contract with a total price chargeable to the customer of £13.2 million.

Year	1	2	3	4	Total
Costs of contract (£m)	2.5	3.5	3.7	2.3	12.0

The profit on the contract is projected to be £1.2 million (i.e., £13.2m – £12m).

To calculate the work-in-progress at the end of a particular year, you need to add up the costs accumulated up to that point in time, giving £2.5m (year 1), £6.0m (year 2), £9.7m (year 3) and £12.0m (year 4). However, because this does not take account of any revenue associated with the contract, the overall profit of the organisation will be artificially low in years 1 to 3 and artificially high in year 4 (when the revenue is recognised on completion of the contract).

To prevent this problem, credit is taken for a proportion of the profit progressively as the work proceeds. For example, you could use a simple arithmetic formula that recognises a proportion of the revenue on the contract each year (as shown in Table 3).

Table 3   Illustration of profit allocation

Year	Costs (£m)	Revenue (£m)	Profit (£m)
1	2.50	2.75	0.25
2	3.50	3.85	0.35
3	3.70	4.07	0.37
4	2.30	2.53	0.23
Total	12.00	13.20	1.20

Activity 3.4

Can you see the basis on which the profit for each year has been calculated? Take a few minutes to think about this.

Feedback

The profit for each year has been calculated as 10 per cent of costs. This was based on the total revenue from the contract being 10 per cent greater than the total costs.

Activity 3.5

Write down why this would be considered an appropriate basis for calculating annual profit on the contract.

If you can think of any reasons why this might not be an appropriate basis, write them down as well.

Feedback

Calculating annual profit on this basis provides a reasonably realistic profit for each year. However, these calculations presuppose:

- first, that the budgeted costs are correct (contracts such as the Channel Tunnel and Edinburgh's Parliament Building demonstrate that this is not always the case)
- second, that the profit at each stage is proportionally related to the costs incurred, which is very rare indeed as long-term contracts inevitably involve some activities that are subsidised by others within the same contract. For example, the first year may be spent planning and preparing for major work to be done later.

No profit, as such, can be earned until something tangible exists that could, if necessary, be given to and used by the customer before the contract is finished. A contract to build a 20 mile motorway could involve building the road in one direction first then, once it is finished, starting on the road going in the other direction. The half finished road could then be opened for traffic while the second half is being built.

To deal with the difficulty of profit recognition on construction projects, for example, the contract value charged to the customer is calculated based on a surveyor's certification of the value of the work completed. The surveyor issues a certificate specifying the amount, and under the contractual terms the customer should pay this sum, less any **retention monies** allowed for in the legal agreement between the parties. Uncertified work refers to the work which has been done by the contractor but not approved by the surveyor. Uncertified work is valued at cost to the contractor. The profit at the end of each year can then be calculated on this more realistic assessment of the value of the contract to that date.

Consider an example of a contract to build a hotel. Assume that work started at the beginning of May 2010. The total contract value is £955,000 (which is the total amount that the customer has agreed to pay for the finished hotel). The contract is expected to be completed at the end of June 2012. The following data are for the year ended 31 March 2011.

	£
Materials delivered and paid for	226,167
Direct labour	56,783
Purchase of equipment	28,403
Site indirect overheads	14,980
Amounts due to suppliers for materials delivered at 31 March 2011	6,458
Inventory at 31 March 2011	43,100

The equipment was bought specifically for this contract and is expected to have a residual value of £8,903 at the end of the work. The value of work certified to date is £275,000. The company's policy on recognising profits is to take credit for 90 per cent of the projected profit on the work certified. The projected costs of the contract in total are estimated to be £857,249.

The contract account at the year end will be as shown in Table 4.

Table 4 Hotel contract account

	£		£
Materials delivered and paid for	226,167	Value of work completed	
Direct labour	56,783	Certified	275,000
Purchase of equipment	28,403	Uncertified work c/d (W3)	19,871
Site indirect overheads	14,980	Inventory c/d	43,100
Amounts due to suppliers for materials delivered	6,458	Equipment c/d (W4)	20,153
Profit (W2)	25,333		
	358,124		358,124

Workings

(W1) Expenditure incurred to 31 March 2011.

	£
Materials delivered and paid for	226,167
Direct labour	56,783
Purchase of equipment	28,403
Site indirect overheads	14,980
Amounts due to suppliers for materials delivered at 31 March 2011	6,458
Total	332,791

(W2) The overall profit on the contract is as follows.

	£
Contract value	955,000
Estimated costs	(857,249)
Projected profit	97,751

The proportion of profit in relation to the work certified is calculated as follows.

$$\frac{£275,000}{£955,000} \times (£97,751 \times 90\%) = £25,333$$

(W3) The value of the uncertified work at 31 March 2011 is calculated as follows.

	£	£
Expenditure incurred to 31 March 2011 (W1)		332,791
Less: Closing inventory	43,100	
Value of equipment (W4)	20,153	
		(63,253)
		269,538
Profit recognised for the period to 31 March 2011		25,333
		294,871
Less: Work certified		(275,000)
Uncertified work in progress		19,871

(W4) The value of the equipment at 31 March 2011 is calculated as follows.

	£
Cost of equipment	28,403
Less: depreciation for 11 months	
$\dfrac{£28,403 - £8,903}{26\,\text{months}} \times 11\,\text{months}$	(8,250)
Value of equipment at 31 March 2011	20,153

Summary

In this session, we have looked at the methods of costing used in activities where work of a non-uniform character is done for a particular customer: job, batch and contract costing. Businesses identify the direct cost of production (costs that can be directly measured in respect of a particular unit of output) and add a share of overheads. Full costing is widely used by business but it is also widely criticised for not providing relevant information. One of the criticisms relates closely to the problem of apportioning total profit between accounting periods.

In the next session, we will look at the fourth widely used approach to costing: process costing.

SESSION **4 Process costing**

Introduction

Upon completion of Session 4, you are expected to be able to:

- explain the nature of process costing
- calculate costs using process costing
- understand the purposes and the problems of process costing.

In this session, you will learn about the nature of process costing and the practical issues that have to be addressed in this approach to costing.

In the previous session, we examined the cost accumulation procedure for a job, a batch and a contract where costs were charged to each individual customer's order, where each order was unique and required different amounts of labour, material and overhead. In this session we will consider the cost accumulation procedure for another system called process costing.

Process costing is used in those industries where the end products are more or less identical. With this type of costing, no attempt is made to allocate the cost to a specific job or batch. Instead, the cost of an individual order for a single unit of product can be obtained by dividing the costs of production for a particular period by the number of units produced during that period.

Our objective here is to examine the cost accumulation procedure that is necessary for inventory valuation and profit measurement under process costing. We will also discuss briefly how cost information should be accumulated for decision making and cost control.

4.1 Process costing

Process costing is used where production moves from one process to the next until final completion. Process costing is applicable where it is not easy to identify separate units of production, for example, food manufacturing and oil refining.

Process costing is a 'form of costing applicable to continuous processes where costs are attributed to the number of units produced. This may involve estimating the number of equivalent units in stock at the start and end of the period under consideration.'

CIMA Official Terminology, p. 10

In comparison, job costing is used in cases where production is carried out against specific orders, mainly to a particular customer's specification. The job acts as the cost unit charged. Under process costing, the procedure for direct costs is the same as for job costing, but with materials and labour being charged to the appropriate process. Process costing is easier to operate than job costing because the detailed work of allocating costs to many individual jobs or batches is unnecessary.

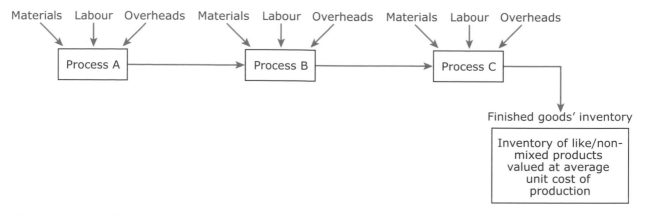

Figure 7 Flow of costs in a process costing system

As you can see from Figure 7, as production moves from process to process, costs are transferred with it. The costs of process A are transferred to process B; process B costs are then added to this cost, and the resulting total cost is transferred to process C; and finally, process C costs are then added to the combined A and B costs. Therefore, the cost becomes cumulative as production proceeds and the addition of the costs from successive processes determines the total cost.

> Process costing is appropriate where identical items are produced continuously. For example, if you know that production costs for a process were £10,000 and 1,000 items were produced the cost per unit can be calculated at £10.

At each stage in the process, an appropriate unit of cost has to be identified. In a typical chemical business this might be the cost per tonne of output. Each process takes into account the opening inventory, to which is added the cost of inputs, including transfers from an earlier process, additional materials, labour costs and expenses. An adjustment is then made for closing inventory. The result is the cost of the product up to that stage in the production process. In addition to the financial values, the process accounts include physical quantities, which can be used to measure the efficiency of the process.

Process losses

In many processes, there is wastage from shrinkage, evaporation and scrap. For example, liquids may evaporate and losses occur in cutting wood to make furniture. Process waste, for example, off-cuts of wood, can sometimes be sold for a small sum. These **normal losses** occur under even efficient operating conditions and cannot be avoided. There are some losses that are not expected to occur, however, under efficient operating conditions. Where resources are inappropriately used, this can result in wastage, giving rise to what are known as **abnormal losses**.

Normal and abnormal losses require a different treatment. The cost of normal losses is absorbed by the units of output produced. Abnormal losses are not included in the process costs but are treated as a general overhead cost for the period and written off to the income statement at the end of the period.

Abnormal losses arise as a result of factors that management ought to be able to control and must be identified and investigated so that effective management action is taken to prevent their recurrence. Examples include the use of inferior raw materials and machine break-downs that cause production to take longer than expected.

When materials are processed they sometimes lose or even gain in volume as a normal result of the process. Engineers can calculate the amount that they expect to lose (normal wastage) or gain, and the rule is to allow for the cost of normal losses in the cost of good production passed on to the next process. Any abnormal losses or gains must be brought to the attention of management and shown as separate charges or credits in the income statement.

Let us now look at an example of unit cost calculations. The application of process costing methods is shown below for a specialist chemical company. The products pass through two stages in the course of production, which are as follows.

Process A	
Materials	11.2 tonnes at a cost of £785 per tonne
Direct production labour	75 hours at £9 per hour
Production expenses	£2,560
Normal wastage	5 per cent of input materials
Output transferred to Process B	10.6 tonnes

Process B	
Materials	9 tonnes at £1,056 per tonne
Direct labour	520 hours at £10.60 per hour
Production expenses	£3,786

Let us look at the Process A account first. We will first construct a schedule of the costs, inputs, and outputs and then check that everything is in balance (i.e., we check to see whether anything unexpected has happened).

Process A	Tonnes	£		Tonnes	£
Materials at £785 per tonne	11.20	8,792	Wastage: normal at 5%	0.56	
Direct labour at £9 per hour × 75 hours		675			
Production expenses		2,560	Transfer to Process B	10.60	12,027
	11.20	12,027		11.16	12,027

As you can see, something has happened – the two sides do not balance. There has been an unexpected loss of 0.04 tonnes in the process. This is an abnormal loss and it must be inserted in the schedule so that the correct values are transferred to the next process.

The revised schedule for Process A as follows.

Process A	Tonnes	£		Tonnes	£
Materials at £785 per tonne	11.20	8,792	Wastage: normal at 5%	0.56	
Direct labour at £9 per hour		675	Wastage: abnormal	0.04	45
Production expenses		2,560	Transfer to Process B	10.60	11,982
	11.20	12,027		11.20	12,027

You can see that Process A has an abnormal wastage with a value of £45. This was found by dividing the total cost of Process A (£12,027) by the total tonnes input minus the normal wastage of five per cent (10.64 tonnes) and multiplying the answer (£1,130 per tonne) by the amount of abnormal wastage (0.04 tonnes). This amount of £45 is shown as a loss in the income statement.

The process cost account for the second stage of production will appear as follows.

Process B	Tonnes	£		Tonnes	£
Transfer from Process A	10.60	11,982	Finished product	19.60	30,784
Materials	9.00	9,504			
Direct labour		5,512			
Production expenses		3,786			
	19.60	30,784		19.60	30,784

Joint products and by-products

A joint product is a separate product resulting from the production of another product manufactured simultaneously by a common series of processing operations. For example, fuel, oil and synthetic rubber are the joint products produced from processing crude oil.

Joint products are 'two or more products produced by the same process and separated in processing, each having a sufficiently high saleable value to merit recognition as a main product.'

CIMA Official Terminology, p. 18

A by-product is produced under the same conditions, but is essentially a secondary result of the process, both in terms of quantity and value of output. In furniture making, for example, by-products include sawdust and wood shavings.

A by-product is an 'output of some value produced incidentally while manufacturing the main product.'

CIMA Official Terminology, p. 7

In many processes, such as chemical production, by-products and joint products are produced. Here the system of process costing has to be designed to account for these products. One of the issues that needs addressing is whether a particular product is a by-product or a joint product.

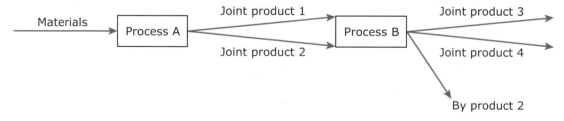

Figure 8   Flow of joint products and by-products

A joint product is considered as the main saleable product and it is normally separately costed. A by-product is not as important as a saleable item and the sale proceeds can be treated as a bonus and shown as an income (with no adjustment for any costs as they have already been assigned to the main product). Alternatively, the process cost account can be credited with the sales value of the by-product at a specific stage in the production process, thus reducing the cost of production to be assigned to the main (joint) products.

A by-product has comparatively low value and is not treated as a product in its own right. A joint product is a separate product, of significant value, resulting from the production of another product.

The methods commonly used to apportion process costs between joint products can be divided into the following two categories.

The **physical measure** method apportions process cost between products in proportion to their volume, for example, weight. Each product is assumed to consume similar amounts of the costs and is therefore charged with its proportionate share of the total cost. This method assumes that the cost per unit is the same for each of the products.

Product	Units produced	Proportion	Joint cost apportioned £	Cost per unit £
A	6,800	34%	34,000	5
B	3,600	18%	18,000	5
C	9,600	48%	48,000	5
Total	20,000	100%	100,000	

The **net realisable value** method apportions process costs between products in proportion to their sales value (minus any further processing costs necessary to enable them to be sold). Process costs are allocated to products in proportion to their sales value, on the assumption that higher sales value indicates higher costs.

Product	Units produced	Sales value £	Proportion of sales value	Joint cost apportioned £
A	6,800	57,000	30%	30,000
B	3,600	38,000	20%	20,000
C	9,600	95,000	50%	50,000
Total	20,000	£190,000	100%	100,000

Process costing with a joint product or by-product has similar purposes to other systems of costing: the cost per unit can be monitored on a regular basis, thus facilitating effective management control; and the degree of accuracy of the average cost is normally sufficient to control operations effectively. Costs ascertained using

'Is that all there is to life – buffalo and buffalo by-products?'

this approach are also likely to be used for pricing and profitability analysis and for inventory valuation when preparing the income statement/profit and loss account and balance sheet.

4.2 Equivalent units

To simplify the discussion of process costing, the problem of opening and closing work-in-progress was initially ignored. Work-in-progress consists of uncompleted units which have not yet consumed the same amount of materials, labour and overhead resources as completed units. Therefore it is misleading, for the purpose of calculating average unit cost, to treat this work-in-progress as fully completed units. Consequently, when opening and closing inventory of work-in-progress exist, unit costs cannot be computed by simply dividing the total cost by the number of units produced. For example, if 9,000 units were started and completed during a period and another 2,000 units were partly completed, then these two items cannot be added together to determine the unit cost. To deal with this, work-in-progress is converted into finished equivalents so that the unit cost can be obtained. For example, materials may be added at the start of the process, so that units would be fully complete as regards materials, whereas labour and overheads may be added throughout the process.

Equivalent units are the result of expressing partly completed units in terms of the stage of completion. To calculate equivalent units for a process at the end of an accounting period, the number of incomplete units is multiplied by the stage of completion at the end of the accounting period.

If the 2,000 partly completed units were 50 per cent complete, we could express this as an equivalent production of 1,000 fully completed units. This would then be added to the completed production of 9,000 units to give a total equivalent production of 10,000 units. The cost per unit can then be calculated. For example, if the costs for the period were £20,000 then the cost per unit completed would be £2, and the total cost would be as follows.

	£
Completed units transferred to next process (9,000 units at £2)	18,000
Work-in-progress (1,000 equivalent units at £2)	2,000
	20,000

Activity 4.1 ....

For Company XYZ, the period data for Process A are as follows.

	Units
Opening work-in-progress	Nil
Units introduced in August	1,000
Units finished	800
Units not completed	200
Materials	£7,000
Labour	£6,000
Overhead	£5,000

It was estimated that, for the 200 incomplete units, the whole of the raw materials had been issued to complete these 200 units. As regards to labour and overhead, they were 50 per cent complete.

Show the unit cost of the process for the month of August and the value at which the completed units should be transferred to Process B.

Feedback

Process cost sheet

	Material	Labour	Overhead
	Units	Units	Units
Opening work-in-progress	–	–	–
Completed	800	800	800
Closing work-in-progress:			
100% material	200		
50% labour		100	
50% overhead			100
Equivalent units	1,000	900	900
Cost for the month	£7,000	£6,000	£5,000
Cost per equivalent unit	£7.00	£6.67	£5.56
Unit cost of process = £19.23			

	Unit cost	
Transferred to Process B		
Completed units (800):		
Material	£7.00	£5,600
Labour	£6.67	£5,336
Overhead	£5.56	£4,448
		£15,384

Closing work-in-progress:		
Material 100% complete	£7.00	£1,400
Labour 50% complete	£6.67	£667
Overhead 50% complete	£5.56	£556
		£2,623

Summary

In this session we have looked at the process costing methods that are widely used in the commercial sectors of the economy. We have examined the cost accumulations necessary for a process costing system where the units of final output are identical. The cost of an individual order for a single unit can be obtained by merely dividing the costs of production for a period by the units produced for that period. We also addressed issues that may arise concerning equivalent units, namely, that in any given inventory of work-in-progress, not all of the elements that make up the total cost may have reached the same degree of completion.

The treatment of normal and abnormal losses has been explained. Normal losses are inherent in the production process and cannot be eliminated. Abnormal losses are avoidable, and the cost of these losses should not be charged to products but written off as a period cost to the income statement.

In Sessions 3 and 4 we have examined four methods of costing which, between them, cover the majority of situations in business and not-for-profit organisations. However, it must be recognised that other costing methods can be developed in particular circumstances. Nevertheless, the underlying basis for collecting and allocating costs will follow principles similar to those we have considered.

SESSION 5 **Activity based costing**

Introduction

Upon completion of Session 5, you will be able to:

- understand the differences between activity based costing (ABC) and other more traditional cost allocation techniques
- understand how indirect costs (overheads) have varying relationships with products
- calculate product costs arising from indirect costs (overheads) using ABC
- understand activity based budgeting (ABB) and activity based management (ABM)
- understand how ABC can be applied to customer or market segment profitability analysis.

So far in your B292 studies, you have learned that traditional costing systems allocate costs to different products on the basis of the volume of units produced – or something closely related to volume, such as the number of direct labour hours or machine hours spent on a particular product. However, many costs arise from activities that are not directly related to the volume of production (i.e., the number of units produced). Allocation of such costs then becomes an issue.

In this session, you will learn how this issue can be addressed through the management accounting procedure of **activity based costing (ABC)**. This session will show how ABC provides a better insight into the cost of producing a product than other more traditional approaches.

5.1 **Why ABC matters**

Activity based costing provides better insight for organisations by:

- linking indirect costs to specific activities involved in production (e.g., the costs of the preparation or 'setting-up' of machinery to produce goods)
- allocating these indirect costs to the final products based upon each product's usage of these activities.

Such indirect, non-volume related activities typically include the ordering and handling of the materials used to produce goods, production scheduling, quality control and the setting-up of machinery.

The following case study illustrates the importance of understanding the costs of running a business.

The British Leyland Mini

In 1977 the ailing UK car company British Leyland (subsequently known as BL) appointed a South African businessman, Michael Edwardes, as Chief Executive.

When Michael Edwardes first met with British Leyland's managers, he asked them for details about the performance of British Leyland and he was told various stories about poor productivity, bad industrial relations and weak financial performance. He then asked them if there was any good news. After some thought, the managers pointed out the huge sales volumes of the Mini – a car that for some years had been one of the best-selling cars in the UK and was exported in large volumes. Michael Edwardes said that this was great news and then he asked the managers about the profits made on the sales of Minis. His question was met with silence until one manager commented that they did not really know. When asked 'why not?' the manager admitted that this was because British Leyland did not know how much it actually cost to make each Mini!

Although this might seem astonishing, such lack of clarity about product costing was always going to be a risk with a company like British Leyland. The Mini was produced at the company's sprawling car plants in the UK – plants which also produced many other (generally less successful) models. With significant overheads and a mixed product output, accurately attributing British Leyland's costs to its units of output (e.g., each Mini) was an exercise fraught with complexity and subjectivity. Yet without accuracy in costing its products, British Leyland was in no position to know how much profit, if any, it was making on one of its best selling cars.

British Leyland's Mini is an example of how lack of knowledge about the costs of running a business (and how much its products actually cost) can impair effective decision making about how products should be priced in order to achieve an acceptable profit margin (or even whether the products should be produced at all).

5.2 The evolution of ABC

Activity based costing did not start to emerge as an academic subject until the late 1980s. By the 1990s it was being adopted, or at least reviewed, by many businesses (Weetman, 2006).

Accounting history sees the evolution of ABC as being a response to the changing pattern of commercial activities in the second half of the 20th century with the emergence of large multi-product businesses with their huge indirect (overhead) costs arising from their extensive infrastructures. Such businesses were far removed from the single product businesses – sometimes operating with limited overheads – which were more typical in industrialised economies until the middle of the 20th century. The challenge for the accountants therefore was how to break down these large indirect (overhead) costs and then fairly allocate them to each product.

Parallel to the growing prevalence of organisations with large indirect costs was the move to lower labour intensity in the production of goods and services. In effect, the replacement of labour with machines provided part of the explanation for the growing size of overheads relative to the outputs of goods and services. Along with growing automation came the development of labour becoming more associated with businesses' service and support functions and less directly associated with production. These developments potentially result in less clarity about the costs arising from producing each product or service.

Some commentators, such as McLaney and Atrill (2008), also see the emergence of ABC as being a reaction to the globalisation of commerce and a greater price awareness of products and services amongst customers. The argument here is that when there is a lack of knowledge about the appropriate prices for products amongst customers or a lack of ability to access products from low-price suppliers (perhaps as a result of trade barriers) it is easier for producers to charge prices to cover the perceived costs of production regardless of the accuracy of cost attribution. Globalisation and a more competitive business environment, together with greater consumer awareness and the reduction of trading barriers, have eroded such market inefficiencies. With more price competitive conditions it is essential for producers to have a full and accurate awareness of production costs. Since consumer awareness and greater competition tighten profit margins, it is vital for businesses to apply accurate cost attribution and effective cost control.

Another factor which has supported the emergence of ABC is the development of computer-based (including PC-based) accounting processes. ABC is more complex (and requires more rigorous data analysis) than traditional cost absorption techniques. Consequently the speed and flexibility afforded to accountants by computerised analysis has supported the adoption of ABC.

So the changing methods of production of goods and services, with a higher proportion of costs being of an indirect nature, and the greater need for certainty in cost attribution due to the more competitive conditions for selling the final products, have made ABC a vital financial discipline for many organisations. The emergence of computer-based data interrogation and accounting processes has supported the application of this new discipline.

5.3 The framework for ABC

Prior to looking at the methodology involved in ABC, we need to establish the framework for undertaking it. Remember that ABC is primarily about the effective allocation of indirect costs (overheads) to the products of a business.

According to McLaney and Atrill (2008):

> 'Historically, businesses have been content to accept overheads exist and, therefore, for costing purposes they must be dealt with in as practical a way as possible. In recent years, however, there has been a growing realisation that overheads do not just happen, but they must be caused by something ...

> Realisation that they (overheads) do not just occur, but that they are caused by activities – such as holding products in stores – that 'drive' the costs, is at the heart of activity based costing (ABC).'

To be able to undertake ABC, the following is required:

- the **classification** of indirect costs relating to the production of a good or service
- the determination of the factors that generate these costs – known as the **cost drivers**.

There are various methods for applying cost classification. One common classification (or 'cost hierarchy') includes the following types of indirect product cost:

1. **Unit level costs** – these are the indirect costs that vary directly with the number of units produced. They include, for example, the costs of using the machines involved in production, such as power costs and 'wear and tear' (and hence eventual replacement) of machine parts.

2. **Batch level costs** – these are costs associated with the processing of multiple units of a particular product. Such costs include, for example, the cost of re-tooling and re-setting machinery to meet the specification requirements of different batches of products. Typically, the greater number of batches, the higher the batch level costs.

A **bill of materials (BOM)** lists all the raw materials and component parts required to assemble a product.

A **routing sheet** is a document that traces the sequence of operations leading to the production of a batch of manufactured components.

3. **Product level costs** – these arise from the services required to support the production of a product. These costs do not usually vary with the number of product units or product batches produced. Such costs include, for example, engineering support, including the maintenance of a bill of materials and a routing sheet.

4. **Facility level costs** – these costs are not attributable to any of a business's individual products. These costs include, for example, the salaries of general management.

(Source: adapted from McWatters et al., 2008)

The four indirect cost classifications set out above range from those which are related to the number of units produced (unit level costs) to those that are simply the costs that need to be incurred to be in business (facility level costs). This raises the issue of how to allocate these costs to individual products. With traditional cost absorption, a single measure of volume is normally used to allocate indirect costs – for example, machine hours or direct labour hours. This, however, risks allocating indirect costs in a way which does not truly reflect how the activity of producing a specific product has actually contributed to indirect costs being incurred. Therefore, we need to identify the 'cost drivers' – the activities that lead to indirect costs being incurred. These cost drivers can take many forms and could include:

- **quality control requirements** – high specification products require more frequent quality control testing (and management supervision) than basic, low specification products.
- **machinery run-time** – some products require more 'run time' on a machine than others.

- **machinery set-up time** – some products require more frequent re-settings of machinery than others. For example, machinery involved in trouser or shoe production will need to be re-set more regularly to accommodate the various size requirements of customers than machinery involved in the production of, say, scarves, ties or belts.

- **product components** – some products comprise more components than others. For products which require many components, it is likely that more time will be spent buying and stocking components than for products which require few (or single) components.

So cost drivers can be used to assign indirect costs to products in a manner that is more forensic (and, hence, accurate) than traditional cost absorption methods. In this way, indirect costs are assigned on the basis of how each productive activity causes such costs to be incurred.

Let us look at a simple example of ABC. An organisation incurs costs of £100,000 per annum in the activity of quality control (much of this amount is due to the salaries of supervisory and quality testing staff). The organisation decides, logically, that the number of quality control tests undertaken should be the basis for allocating this cost to individual products. If, during the course of the year, the organisation undertakes 8,000 quality control tests, the average cost of a single test is £100,000/8,000 = £12.50 per test. This means that each product will be assigned £12.50 for each quality control test it requires. High specification products will require more quality control tests and therefore absorb more of these related costs than low specification products which require less quality control testing.

As shown in Figure 9, ABC estimates the cost of producing products. ABC determines the cost of each activity involved in production and what gives rise to each cost (i.e., the cost driver). ABC then determines how each individual product is responsible for incurring the cost of these activities required for its production – the 'activity cost driver'.

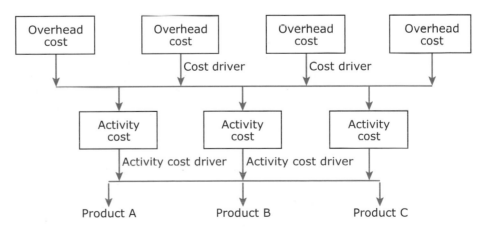

Figure 9 ABC cost allocations

5.4 Examples of ABC

We will now look at an example of ABC, using the framework we examined in Section 5.3.

All Soles is a small company which manufactures a range of footwear from slippers to fashionable boots for men and women. The indirect costs of the activities associated with All Soles footwear production are shown in the following table. These exclude the direct costs of production, such as the cost of materials.

	£
Purchasing	120,000
Setting-up machinery	240,000
Quality control	100,000
Machining	480,000
Total cost	940,000

The activities of purchasing, setting-up machinery, quality control and machining are therefore the cost drivers that generate the indirect costs.

The following table shows the units of output of each product and the aggregate requirement of each product for the activities of purchasing, setting-up, quality control and machining.

	Number of units	Purchasing transactions	Machine set-ups	Quality inspections	Machine hours
Slippers	10,000	500	200	50	200
Sandals	20,000	1,200	400	50	800
Shoes	115,000	3,800	1,400	650	4,500
Boots	5,000	500	400	250	500
Total	150,000	6,000	2,400	1,000	6,000

From this data we can calculate the cost of each activity as follows.

Purchasing	£120,000/6,000 transactions	= £20 per transaction
Set-ups	£240,000/2,400 set-ups	= £100 per set-up
Quality inspections	£100,000/1,000 inspections	= £100 per inspection
Machining	£480,000/6,000 machine hours	= £80 per machine hour

Now we know how much these activities cost and how each product has driven the volume of each of these activities, the costs (indirect) that can be allocated to each of the four products can be determined. The following table sets out the calculations for slippers. The same methodology should then be applied to sandals, shoes and boots.

	Slippers	Sandals	Shoes	Boots	Total
	£	£	£	£	£
Purchasing (500 × £20) =	10,000	24,000	76,000	10,000	120,000
Set-ups (200 × £100) =	20,000	40,000	140,000	40,000	240,000
Quality control (50 × £100) =	5,000	5,000	65,000	25,000	100,000
Machining (200 × £80) =	16,000	64,000	360,000	40,000	480,000
Total	51,000	133,000	641,000	115,000	940,000
Number of units produced	10,000	20,000	115,000	5,000	
Cost per unit	£5.10	£6.65	£5.57	£23.00	

Another way to represent indirect costs per unit is shown in the following table which, once again, sets out the calculations for slippers. The same methodology should then be applied to sandals, shoes and boots.

	Slippers	Sandals	Shoes	Boots
	£	£	£	£
Purchasing (£10,000/10,000) =	1.00	1.20	0.66	2.00
Set-ups (£20,000/10,000) =	2.00	2.00	1.22	8.00
Quality control (£5,000/10,000) =	0.50	0.25	0.57	5.00
Machining (£16,000/10,000) =	1.60	3.20	3.13	8.00
Total	5.10	6.65	5.58*	23.00

* rounding difference of £0.01 from £5.57 in the previous table.

The total indirect costs per unit provide some interesting – although not entirely surprising – observations. Generally, the costs per unit rise when the product being made is more complex. Boots are more complex to produce than slippers and, per unit, the absorption of indirect costs is therefore greater. For example, per unit, more time will be spent purchasing materials, machine set-ups will be more numerous, and the need for quality control will be greater, proportionately.

This relationship between product complexity and the absorption of indirect costs is not always going to be entirely linear though, as shown by the absorption per unit of shoes being less than for sandals. This arises because the large output of shoes generates some economies of scale in the need for the activities (e.g., machine set-ups) which generate the indirect costs.

Once the direct costs are added, the management of All Soles will be informed about the overall cost per unit of each item of footwear. They will therefore be positioned to make effective pricing decisions for the sale of their products. Indeed, the detailed breakdown in costs and information about the profitability of each of their product range, will assist management in making decisions about their best product mix, such as whether the production of certain items should be curtailed due to their lack of profitability. This shows that an effective ABC has the potential to be a powerful management tool.

In the following activity, you will look at ABC in the context of a service organisation.

Activity 5.1 ....

This activity looks at how ABC applies to an educational institution which has three faculties (Humanities, Mathematics and Arts) that create courses which are used by schools and colleges.

In the process of creating courses, specific activities which generate indirect costs are:

- copyright services (the department which obtains permissions for the course texts to use materials compiled by external authors)
- editorial services (the department which converts the draft course texts into the finished product)
- IT services (used by the internal authors to research the course content and draft it).

	£
Copyright services	80,000
Editorial services	450,000
IT services	240,000
Total cost	770,000

The following table shows the units of output of each faculty (i.e., courses) and the aggregate requirement of each faculty for copyright clearances, editing and IT services.

Faculty	Number of courses	Copyright permission requests	Editorial cycles*	IT usage (hours)
Humanities	20	500	80	20,000
Mathematics	5	10	40	3,000
Arts	10	290	30	7,000
Total	35	800	150	30,000

* the number of drafts that are edited before the course texts are completed.

Calculate the indirect costs to be allocated to each of the three faculties (in respect of the courses they are responsible for) and prepare a schedule of activity component costs per course (i.e., per unit of each faculty's courses).

Feedback ....

The cost of each activity is as follows.

Copyrights	£80,000/800 requests	= £100 per request
Editorial services	£450,000/150 cycles	= £3,000 per cycle
IT services	£240,000/30,000 hours	= £8 per hour

Now that we know how much each activity costs and how each product has driven the volume of each of these activities, the costs (indirect) of producing the courses can be allocated to each of the three faculties. The following table sets out the calculations for the Humanities faculty. The same methodology should also be applied to the Mathematics and Arts faculties.

	Humanities	Mathematics	Arts	Total
	£	£	£	£
Copyrights (500 x £100) =	50,000	1,000	29,000	80,000
Editing (80 x £3,000) =	240,000	120,000	90,000	450,000
IT Services (20,000 x £8) =	160,000	24,000	56,000	240,000
Total	450,000	145,000	175,000	770,000
Number of courses Produced	20	5	10	
Cost per course	£22,500	£29,000	£17,500	

The activity costs per unit (i.e., each course) are shown in the following table which sets out the calculations for the Humanities faculties. The same methodology should also be applied to the Mathematics and Arts faculties.

	Humanities	Mathematics	Arts
	£	£	£
Copyrights (£50,000/20) =	2,500	200	2,900
Editing (£240,000/20) =	12,000	24,000	9,000
IT Services (£160,000/20) =	8,000	4,800	5,600
Total	22,500	29,000	17,500

5.5 The benefits of ABC and new developments in cost management

So far we have examined the background to the evolution of ABC and the methodology for applying it in both the manufacturing and service sectors. In this section, we will review the purported benefits of ABC and examine how this approach to cost accounting has laid the foundation for further developments to cost accounting and control, such as:

- activity based budgeting (ABB)
- activity based management (ABM)
- customer account profitability analysis.

5.5.1 The benefits of ABC

The examination of the evolution of ABC and our subsequent exploration of the framework and methodology for its execution highlight the key benefit that ABC brings to management – the ability to link costs effectively to products. This is a crucial starting point for knowing what minimum prices a business should be charging for its products. Therefore, ABC is an essential requirement for product pricing and profit margin management.

Of course market conditions may mean that a business is unable to charge the minimum price for its products – conditions may be too price competitive for costs to be covered. However, ABC can assist managers with this. At the very least, effective ABC will highlight where product ranges should be dropped to avoid loss making activities. Alternatively, the determination of the differential profits made on different products will provide guidance on how to alter the product mix to enhance profitability.

ABC also facilitates effective cost control since it highlights where the cost drivers are and, hence, pinpoints where management action can be taken to improve product profitability.

For example, the educational institution we examined in Activity 5.1 may find that under current cost conditions its Mathematics courses are unprofitable and can only be priced at levels which competitors can undercut. However, if the ABC cost drivers are examined, there could be scope to drive down the cost of each course. Areas to look at might include:

- Could the number of external sources being used in the course texts be reduced, thus reducing copyright clearance costs?

- Could the number of iterations to the editorial team be reduced by improving the quality of the first drafts of the course texts, or by the editorial team adopting a shortened cycle for completion of the course texts?

- Could the usage of IT facilities be reduced – or, perhaps, outsourced at a lower cost – to reduce that component of indirect costs?

Essentially then, effective ABC enables organisations to be aware of their current cost versus price (and hence profitability) position. ABC also highlights where an organisation can alter existing production practices to drive down costs and enhance profit margins.

Indeed, just the process of undertaking ABC and reviewing the outcomes illuminates how an organisation operates. ABC can demonstrate how the different parts of an organisation link together and clarifies the flows of activities from the start of processes to the delivery of final products and services. Such analysis can be of considerable help in identifying weaknesses in the business structure – for example, where unnecessary costs are being incurred or where there are 'bottlenecks' in the production processes.

Therefore, ABC can enable managers to know more about how their organisation's work and where operational improvements can be made.

5.5.2 Activity based budgeting

The adoption of ABC has led to certain spin-off developments in the ways that organisations undertake financial control.

The first of these is **activity based budgeting (ABB)**. Since ABC views organisations as comprising an inter-linked series of activities, a consequential development has been that budgets should be divided up between these activities rather than, say, departments. The collective result is an activity driven budget.

After the emergence of ABC, a framework for ABB was developed by Brimson and Fraser (1990). This is summarised in Figure 10.

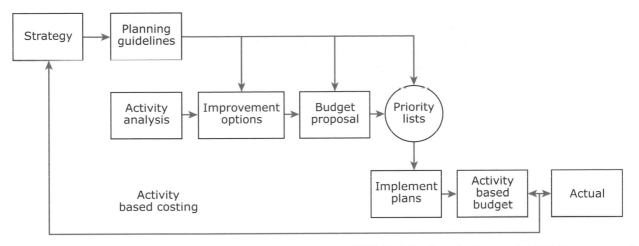

Figure 10 The ABB process. Source: Brimson & Fraser (1991). 'The key features of ABB'. Management Accounting, Volume 69, Issue 1, p. 42.

The methodology of ABB exemplifies certain benefits of ABC referred to in Section 5.5.1. Drawing up an activity based budget shows the linkages between the activities that comprise an organisation's operation and makes the cost drivers visible. By setting out how much each activity costs, a focus can be provided on where there may be inefficiencies and scope for cost reductions (or what Brimson and Fraser refer to as 'improvement options').

5.5.3 Activity based management

The second spin-off from ABC (and ABB) is **activity based management (ABM)**. This is where activity based costing becomes the basis for management and control.

In addition to applying the cost management and control practices that derive from the use of ABC, activity based management stretches these practices further by reviewing and altering the following:

- operational processes
- product mixes
- product prices
- customer relationships.

ABM does more than analysing the costs of activities – it extends to the wider management and strategy of an organisation and its relationship with its customers. ABM is supported by what is known as **value chain analysis**. This breaks down the activities of the business between those that give value to the customer from purchasing the organisation's products or services (**value added activities**) and those that do not (**non-value added activities**).

Figure 11 shows the value added activities of two value chains: a footwear company called All Soles (a) and an academic institution which produces courses (b). These examples were discussed in Section 5.4.

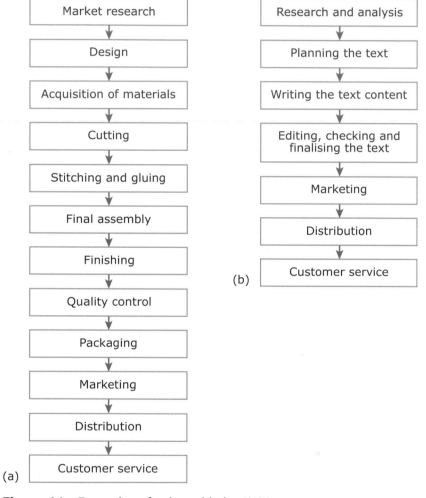

Figure 11   Examples of value added activities

Each value added activity in Figure 11 is critical to satisfying customers. The implication of ABM is that an organisation should focus on maximising cost efficiency and the quality of its value added activities.

Non-value added activities of value chains, such as administration and inventory management, do not have a direct impact upon the customer or the value they perceive as getting from an organisation's product or service. Whilst they are essential parts of running an organisation, the fact that they have no direct benefit to the customer implies that robust cost management of such activities should be exerted under ABM.

5.5.4 Customer account profitability analysis

The analysis of ABC undertaken in Section 5.4 examined the costs arising from producing products and services. The analysis stopped at the point that production was completed. However, in recent years, activity based analysis has extended to the examination of the costs of undertaking business with different categories of customer.

How does this form of ABC work? The key difference is that rather than focussing on the product as the unit of analysis, the cost 'object' is actually the customer (or customer type) or the market segment an organisation is selling to. The cost drivers under this approach to ABC include:

- supply and delivery costs
- the quality requirements sought by customers
- sales and promotion costs
- after-sales service
- price discounts.

The key point is that customers with similar volumes of purchases may consume different amounts of services and support resources.

By allocating costs to customers or market segments rather than just products, an organisation can start to determine which are profitable and which are loss-making. **Customer profitability** is defined as the difference between the revenues earned from a customer relationship and the costs associated with that relationship. The findings that arise are potentially powerful management information since they will highlight where customer relationships should be curtailed or renegotiated (i.e., where they are currently loss-making) and further developed (i.e., where they generate profits). In this way, an organisation knows where it needs to focus its sales in order to maximise profits. It will also learn where it may have to change the pricing of its products and services for different categories of customer.

This methodology is of great practical benefit to organisations selling services to market segments that can be clearly delineated. Certainly the approach can be used by, for example, financial services organisations to determine which customers to focus on (e.g., so-called 'high net-worth' customers). Lower income customers, undertaking limited transactions, but still incurring account management costs, may be a group with whom that financial organisations conduct business, but only in a limited way.

The process of applying ABC in this manner is complex and, to a degree, subjective. Apportioning indirect costs amongst customer groups is a demanding process and it is challenging to apply costs fairly and accurately.

Organisations undertaking this customer based approach to ABC also need to consider more than just the short term when making decisions about customer relationships. Non-profitable relationships today may become very profitable in future. A classic example of this is the provision of banking services to students. These banking services may be unprofitable in the short term, but over time, as students graduate and eventually move into high income jobs, the relationships become profitable with a range of products and services being sold to graduates. Therefore, customer based activity cost analysis needs to incorporate a **lifetime analysis** of customer profitability to be a truly effective financial management tool.

Customer account profitability analysis is a relatively new and emergent strand of ABC. As Guilding and McManus (2002) noted, this is consistent with 'a growing tendency for businesses to seek competitive advantage by applying customer-focused strategies.'

Activity 5.2 ....

Apart from the potential longer term benefits identified using 'lifetime analysis', why might an organisation maintain a customer relationship which was not profitable?

Feedback ....

Sometimes loss-making relationships are maintained because an organisation may imminently expect to undertake new areas of business with the customer which will make the relationship profitable. Alternatively the customer may be prestigious and the association with this particular customer may lead to marketing and publicity benefits for the organisation.

5.6 The limitations of ABC

ABC has been adopted by many organisations in order to allocate and manage indirect costs effectively and to improve relationships with their customers and market segments. However, ABC does have some limitations:

- Typically, ABC extends only to the point at which the production of a good or service is completed. In effect, ABC often stops at the 'factory door'. However, organisations (especially those engaged in customer profitability analysis) are increasingly extending ABC into costs arising from marketing, sales and after-sales service.

- The allocation of indirect costs (overheads) to products via cost drivers often involves some subjectivity or simplification. For example, in the 'All Soles' example in Section 5.4, we assumed that each quality control test absorbed the same resource regardless of the type of footwear involved. This was a simplification, since testing boots should take longer (per unit of product) than testing slippers. This issue can be addressed by being more detailed in the way indirect costs are assigned to products. However, this would require more time and detailed systems of analysis and would add to the cost of undertaking ABC. The risk is that the systems and personnel required to conduct ABC on a forensic basis would result in ABC procedures becoming material indirect costs in themselves. The consequence is that the application of ABC generates additional costs which then have to be allocated to each category of product or service! Indeed, research indicates that those organisations which have not adopted ABC after a cost-benefit analysis act this way because the benefits of the additional information obtained do not outweigh the additional costs incurred in obtaining the information.

Typically, this has been found to be the case where indirect costs account for less than 15 per cent of total costs.

- Some debate also exists about the allocation of labour costs of production to individual products. Such costs may be seen as being akin to raw material costs in that they are direct and therefore fall outside the processes of ABC. However, some organisations may view labour costs as being a production overhead, meaning that ABC should apply when determining the allocation of labour costs to products.

Summary

In this session we have looked at activity based costing (ABC), activity based budgeting (ABB) and activity based management (ABM). We have looked at how they can lead to a better understanding of an organisation and thereby provide potential improvements to organisational costing, planning, control and decision making.

The organisations which are most likely to benefit from the adoption of ABC and ABM are those:

- operating in highly competitive markets, where the need for accurate production cost data is paramount
- with diverse products, processes and customers
- with significant indirect costs relative to total costs
- where the consumption of resources by the production of individual products or customers is not proportional to the volume of production (a circumstance typical of a new technology industry or an industry with a strong customer service culture).

More accurate product costs can lead organisations to a better product mix and improved pricing decisions. Additionally, the analysis of activities and their costs which ABC provides can lead to better decisions about cost reduction opportunities, more efficient supplier relationships, and a greater focus on offering value to customers.

Unit summary

In this unit, we have looked at inventory management and the principles of the reorder level method of inventory control were covered. We looked at how to calculate the economic order quantity for an organisation when provided with appropriate information, including potential discounts. We also considered JIT inventory management.

This unit has also explained the advantages of integrated accounting systems over separate systems for cost and financial accounting. Most modern cost accounting systems are integrated systems, incorporating coding systems which allow data to be analysed and presented in different ways for management and external financial reporting purposes.

In a commercial context we relate the cost of a product or service to the revenue it generates in order to make an informed judgement about profit. Similarly, in the public sector and other not-for-profit organisations, an understanding of cost and its identification and measurement is an essential component for assessing whether the resources are being used in the most effective and efficient way. While cost seems to be a very simple concept, its accurate determination can be a complex matter, involving the analysis of considerable amounts of data, as well as requiring the exercise of judgement to ensure that the resulting cost figures are relevant to the organisation's needs.

Accounting for costs requires the identification of suitable cost units and a supporting accounting system. A range of costing methods was considered, from job costing to activity based costing systems. The methods described in this unit are the most widely used but there are others that are tailored to the specific needs of an organisation.

The methods covered in this unit are the main approaches used by management accountants. They provide a practical framework for ascertaining costs. You must realise that there is a degree of subjectivity in their application, such as the challenge in contract costing about how profit is calculated and, in job costing, about the way in which indirect costs are apportioned. The need to use an appropriate approach when establishing cost cannot be over-emphasised as the following anecdotal tale illustrates.

It is said that one of the reasons why Lord Leverhulme, the soap manufacturer, was so successful was because of his accounting treatment of a by-product from the process of soap making. In the process of treating the raw material, glycerine is produced. The other soap makers of his day treated the sale proceeds of this as a bonus but Lord Leverhulme deducted this income from the cost of his soap. His costing system resulted in a lower net cost for the product, which was reflected in a more competitive selling price, which led to the demise of many of his competitors.

The moral of this story is that you should ensure that you understand how costs are calculated and use appropriate and relevant theoretical concepts when calculating costs.

Having completed this unit, you should now have a clear idea of the different ways in which costs can be calculated and charged to units produced or services provided.

Overall, you should now be able to *explain* what costing is and be ready to start looking at the 'bigger picture', namely, how the costs identified are used in practice – including in the process of budgeting, which is the subject of Unit 4. You should now be able to:

- *make* specific recommendations to an organisation so that it can improve its inventory management
- *describe* the just-in-time approach to inventory management
- *understand* and *apply* the principles of double-entry bookkeeping to costing
- *prepare* a set of integrated accounts
- *explain* and *calculate* costs using the job, batch and contract costing methods of costing
- *explain* and *calculate* the cost of a product or service from basic information using process costing
- *explain* the difference between activity based costing and the more traditional approaches to costing units of production or service.

Self-assessed Questions

These SAQs are designed to give you additional practice at answering questions covering material in this unit. Some are shorter than typical examination questions might be, or of a type not found in examinations (e.g., SAQ 4, SAQ 5 and SAQ 10).

Question 1

The following information relates to a particular item of stock held during an accounting period.

Opening stock	Quantity	Total cost (£)
FIFO	156	1,716
LIFO	156	1,638
Average cost	156	1,690

During the period, the following goods were received from suppliers.

Delivery	Quantity	Total cost (£)
First	324	3,434
Second	196	2,156
Third	220	2,464

Goods issued to production were *all* issued after the third delivery was received.

Issued	Quantity
First	210
Second	150

Calculate the cost of goods charged to production and the closing stock valuation based on the following methods of stock valuation.

(a) FIFO

(b) LIFO

(c) Average cost.

Suggested answer ....

	Charge to production (£)	Closing stock valuation (£)
(a) FIFO	3,878	5,892
(b) LIFO	4,004	5,688
(c) Average cost	3,915	5,829

(a) *FIFO*: the 210 issued comprises 156 from opening stock plus 54 from the first delivery = £1,716 + (54 × (£3,434 ÷ 324)) = £2,288. The 150 issued were all from the first delivery = 150 × (£3,434 ÷ 324) = £1,590. The total charge to production = £2,288 + £1,590 = £3,878. The quantity of stock left was 536: 120 from the first delivery (£1,272) plus all the second (£2,156) and third (£2,464) deliveries = £5,892.

(b) *LIFO*: the 210 issued are all from the third delivery = 210 × (£2,464 ÷ 220) = £2,352. Of the 150, 10 were issued from the third delivery = 10 × (£2,464 ÷ 220) = £112; and the other 140 were from the second delivery = 140 × (£2,156 ÷ 196) = £1,540, making a total of £112 + £1,540 = £1,652 for the 150. The total charge to production = £2,352 + £1,652 = £4,004. The quantity of stock left was 536: 56 from the second delivery (£616) plus all the first delivery (£3,434) and all the opening stock (£1,638) = £5,688.

(c) *Average cost*: after the third delivery, there were 896 in stock at a total cost of £9,744. The total issued was 360 items of stock at £9,744 ÷ 896 each = £3,915. The quantity of stock left was 536 at £9,744 ÷ 896 each = £5,829.

Question 2 ....

Biscay is a wholesaler which buys and sells a wide range of products, one being a hair-dryer. The company sells 140,000 hair-dryers each year at a unit price of £20. Sales follow an even pattern throughout the year. Biscay buys its hair-dryers from one supplier in batches of 14,000 for £15 each hair-dryer. The most recent invoice from the supplier was as follows.

	£
Cost of 14,000 at £15 per hair-dryer in the batch	210,000
Delivery cost of 14,000 at 20p per hair-dryer in the batch	2,800
Administration charge per order	2,000
	214,800

Recently, Biscay has carried out a costing exercise. It estimates that each order it places costs the organisation a total of £1,750 in terms of administration and quality control sample checks.

The hair-dryers are stored in a warehouse rented by the organisation on an annual basis. Space in the warehouse costs £8 per square metre per annum and each hair-dryer occupies 0.25 square metres. Assume (for the purpose of this question) that rental cost is a variable cost dependent on space taken up and is not a period, that is, fixed cost. In addition to the warehouse rental, Biscay pays £8 per year per hair-dryer for other holding costs, including warehouse wages.

(a) Using the variables in the EOQ formula you learned, identify the ordering costs per order and holding costs per unit per annum for the hair-dryers.

(b) Complete the following table and use it to plot a graph of order size against cost, showing the ordering costs and holding costs for a range of order sizes or quantities in the course of a year based upon the even annual demand of 140,000. (Hint: the holding cost per order size is simple to work out as it is merely the holding cost per unit multiplied by average amount of units in inventory. The order cost is more complicated as it depends upon how many orders are needed to fulfil the demand).

Order size x	Annual holding cost (£) $\frac{Hx}{2}$	Annual order cost (£) $\frac{DC}{x}$
4,000		
6,000		
8,000		
10,000		
12,000		
14,000		
16,000		
18,000		

(c) Use a graph to identify the economic order quantity.

(d) Use the EOQ formula to confirm the economic order quantity for the hair-dryers that you identified in (c).

Suggested answer ....

(a) If 'C' is the cost of placing an order, C = £2,000 (what the supplier charges on each order) + £1,750 (what the organisation estimates each order costs 'internally'). Therefore, C = £3,750.

The order cost (where 'x' is the number of units in an order) = (DC)/x. If D = 140,000 and C = £3,750, when x = 4,000, the order cost = (140,000 × £3,750)/4,000

For the holding costs, 'H', each hair-dryer needs 0.25 square metres of space and therefore costs £8 × 0.25 = £2 to hold for a year. Adding on the other holding costs of £8 per unit, we get a holding cost per unit per annum of:

H = £2 + £8 = £10.

(b)

Order size x	Holding cost (£)	Order cost (£)
4,000	20,000	131,250
6,000	30,000	87,500
8,000	40,000	65,625
10,000	50,000	52,500
12,000	60,000	43,750
14,000	70,000	37,500
16,000	80,000	32,813
18,000	90,000	29,167

Working

Annual holding cost at 4,000 order size = Average number of units being held × holding costs per unit per annum

= (4,000/2) × £10, etc.

Annual order cost at 4,000 order size = No. of orders × costs per order

= (140,000/4,000) × £3,750, etc.

(c) You can see from the graph that as the average inventory level or the order quantity increases, the holding cost also increases. Alternatively, the ordering costs decline as inventory level and order quantities are increased. The total cost line represents the sum of both holding and the ordering costs and indicates where total cost is at a minimum. In Figure 12 this is at about 10,250 units.

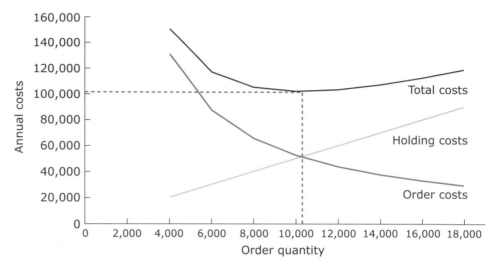

Figure 12   Order size and holding costs

(d) $EOQ = \sqrt{\dfrac{2CD}{H}} = \sqrt{\dfrac{2 \times £3,750 \times 140,000}{£10}} = 10,246.95$ units

(which would be rounded up to 10,247 units).

Question 3

Biscay, the company in SAQ 2, has been offered a 2 per cent discount on the cost of the hair-dryers if it places orders in quantities of 18,000.

Should it accept the discount and place larger orders?

Suggested answer

Per the answer to part (d) in SAQ 2, the total costs for Biscay if it orders the EOQ of 10,247 units are:

				£
Cost of buying the hairdryers	=	£15 × 140,000	=	2,100,000
Cost of ordering	=	(140,000/10,247) × £3,750	=	51,235
Cost of holding	=	(£10 × 10,247)/2	=	51,235
				2,202,470

The total costs for Biscay if it orders 18,000 units are:

				£
Cost of buying the hairdryers	=	£15 × 140,000 × 0.98	=	2,058,000
Cost of ordering	=	(140,000/18,000) × £3,750	=	29,167
Cost of holding	=	(£10 × 18,000)/2	=	90,000
				2,177,167

Ordering 18,000 units will, therefore, save £2,202,470 − £2,177,167 = £25,303 over a year. As expected, the holding cost increases (from £51,235 to £90,000), but this is more than compensated by the reduced cost of buying and ordering. Biscay should take the discount.

Question 4

What are the principal differences between JIT inventory management and more traditional inventory control systems?

Use the table below to prepare your answer. Consider JIT and traditional systems from the view point of supplier and buyer (customer).

	JIT	Traditional inventory control systems
Purchase size		
Supplier selection		
Inspection		
Negotiation		
Transport		
Paperwork		
Packaging		

Suggested answer

A comparison of JIT and more traditional inventory control systems.

	JIT	Traditional inventory control systems
Purchase size	Small and frequent	Large
Supplier selection	Single source	Multiple sources
	Long-term contract Local	Short- and long-term contract
Inspection	Rely on supplier	Buyer is responsible
Negotiation	To achieve quality and reliability at a 'fair' price	To achieve best price (and delivery)
Transport	Determined by buyer	Left to supplier
Paperwork	Minimal	Large amounts
Packaging	Small, standard, well marked containers	Left to supplier

Question 5 ....

Does your organisation, or one with which you are familiar, use any form of JIT approaches?

Whether it does or not, what do you think would be the potential benefits to this particular organisation of such techniques?

You may find it helpful to read the article by Johnson (2004) 'Just-in-time operations and backflush accounting' in ACCA's *Accounting & Business*. This can be downloaded from the B292 website.

Question 6 ....

The Manufacturing Company Ltd is using absorption costing methods and the following specific production and cost data are available for a given period.

- Raw (direct) materials costing £1,200,000 were acquired on credit.

- Materials costing £1,000,000 were issued to work-in-progress.

- Direct wages amounted to £600,000.

- Variable overheads should be £0.50 per unit, and fixed overheads will be £1,120,000. At an assumed output level of 560,000 units, a fixed overhead absorption rate is £2 per unit.

- At the end of the period, the fixed overhead amounted to £1,060,000, and variable overhead to £380,000.

- Units actually produced amounted to 600,000.

- The total cost of completed production was £2,400,000.

Using the information given above for this period, you are required to prepare the following integrated accounts:

- materials

- work-in-progress

- finished goods

- wages

- variable and fixed overheads.

Suggested answer ....

Materials

	£'000		£'000
Material received from supplier	1,200	Work-in-progress	1,000
		Balance c/d	200
	1,200		1,200
Balance b/d	200		

Wages

	£'000		£'000
Total wages paid	600	Work-in-progress	600

Variable overhead

	£'000		£'000
Creditors/Bank	380	Work-in-progress	300
		Income statement	80
	380		380

Fixed overhead

	£'000		£'000
Creditors/Bank	1,060	Work-in-progress	1,200
Income statement	140		
	1,200		1,200

Work-in-progress

	£'000		£'000
Material	1,000	Finished goods	2,400
Wages	600	Balance c/d	700
Variable overhead	300		
Fixed overhead	1,200		
	3,100		3,100
Balance b/d	700		

Finished goods

	£'000		£'000
Work-in-progress	2,400	Balance c/d	2,400
Balance b/d	2,400		

Question 7

A building company uses a system of job costing to calculate costs and profits on individual jobs. It is doing a variety of jobs for its customers. The following information, extracted from the costing records, relates to jobs completed during one particular month.

	Job 11	Job 14	Job 16
Materials used	£16,219	£17,154	£4,829
Direct labour hours	450	390	208
Other direct expenses	£1,290	£954	£292
Charge to customer	£25,320	£24,970	£9,850

The direct labour hour wage rate is £11.20.

The indirect costs for the period amount to £5,250 and the total of direct labour hours on all contracts is 2,436. Indirect costs should be charged to jobs on the basis of direct labour hours.

Calculate the costs of each of the jobs and the profit on each job.

Suggested answer

The costs and profitability of the jobs are as follows.

	Job 11	Job 14	Job 16
	£	£	£
Charge to customer	25,320	24,970	9,850
Materials used	(16,219)	(17,154)	(4,829)
Direct labour	(5,040)	(4,368)	(2,330)
Other direct expenses	(1,290)	(954)	(292)
Indirect costs	(972)	(842)	(449)
Total costs	(23,521)	(23,318)	(7,900)
Net profit	1,799	1,652	1,950

Note: Indirect costs are charged to jobs at a rate of £2.16 per direct labour hour. This rate is based on the total indirect costs for the period and the total direct labour hours for the period (£5,250 ÷ 2,436).

Question 8

Work started on a contract to build a ship at the beginning of July 2012.

The total contract value is £644,000. The contract is expected to be completed at the end of September 2014. The following data relate to the year ended 31 March 2013.

	£
Materials delivered and paid for	160,000
Direct labour	72,000
Purchase of equipment	10,000
Site indirect overheads	18,000
Amounts due to suppliers for materials delivered at 31 March 2013	56,000
Inventory at 31 March 2013	64,000

The equipment was bought specifically for this contract and is expected to have a residual value of £4,000 at the end of the work. The value of work certified to date is £140,000. The company's policy on recognising profits is to take credit for 100 per cent of the projected profit on the work certified. The projected costs of the contract in total are estimated to be £524,000.

Prepare:

(a)   the ship contract account at 31 March 2013

(b)   the estimated costs for the remainder of the contract.

Suggested answer ....

You need to do this question in stages.

(1) Prepare the ship contract account and enter all the figures you have been given in the question. You will not have a figure for profit, uncertified work or equipment.

(2) Calculate the profit figure for the period and enter it in the ship contract account.

(3) Calculate the equipment figure and enter it in the ship contract account.

(4) The uncertified work figure is the difference between the two sides of the account. However, you need to check it by calculating it. To do so, you must first calculate the expenditure for the year. Do not forget to include amounts you have not yet paid to your suppliers.

- Subtract closing inventory and the value of the equipment from the expenditure figure and add the profit for the period.

- Deduct the value of work certified. What you have left is the value of the uncertified work-in-progress.

(5) Check that the figure that you have just calculated is the same as the balancing figure needed for the ship contract account. If it is not, then you will have made a mistake.

(a)

Ship contract account at 31 March 2013

	£		£
Materials delivered and paid for	160,000	Value of work completed	
Direct labour	72,000	Certified	140,000
Purchase of equipment	10,000	Uncertified work c/d (W2)	130,087
Site indirect overheads	18,000	Inventory c/d	64,000
Amounts due to suppliers for materials delivered	56,000	Equipment c/d (W3)	8,000
Profit (W1)	26,087		
	342,087		342,087

(b) The calculation of estimated costs for the remainder of the contract is as follows.

	£	£
Total projected costs		524,000
Materials delivered and paid for	160,000	
Direct labour	72,000	
Purchase of equipment	10,000	
Site indirect overheads	18,000	
Amounts due to suppliers for materials delivered	56,000	
		(316,000)
		208,000
Less: residual value of equipment		(4,000)
		204,000

Workings

Expenditure for the year, including amounts still unpaid, is calculated as follows.

	£
Materials delivered and paid for	160,000
Direct labour	72,000
Purchase of equipment	10,000
Site overheads	18,000
Creditors for materials delivered	56,000
	316,000

(W1) The calculation of the overall profit on the contract is as follows.

	£
Contract value	644,000
Estimated costs	(524,000)
Projected profit	120,000

The profit relating to the work certified is:

$$\frac{£140,000}{£644,000} \times (£120,000 \times 100\%) = 26,087$$

(W2) The value of the uncertified work at 31 March 2013 is calculated as follows:

	£	£
Expenditure incurred to 31 March 2013		316,000
Less: Closing inventory	64,000	
Value of equipment (W3)	8,000	
		(72,000)
		244,000
Profit recognised for the period to 31 March 2013		26,087
		270,087
Less: Work certified		(140,000)
Uncertified work in progress		130,087

(W3) The value of the equipment at 31 March 2013 is calculated as follows.

	£
Cost of equipment	10,000
Less: depreciation for 9 months:	
$\frac{(£10,000 - £4,000)}{27 \text{ months}} \times 9 \text{ months}$	(2,000)
Value of equipment at 31 March 2013	8,000

Question 9 ....

What are the principal differences between specific order costing (job, batch and contract costing) and process costing?

Use the table below to prepare your answer.

	Specific order costing			Process costing
	Job costing	*Batch costing*	*Contract costing*	
Applies to				
Fxamples				
Features				

Suggested answer ....

	Specific order costing			Process costing
	Job costing	*Batch costing*	*Contract costing*	
Applies to	Work done to a customer's specific requirements.	Identical items manufactured in batches.	Work of significant value usually lasting more than one financial accounting period.	One or more processes continually producing items.
Examples	Car repair, landscaping a garden.	Cakes in a bakery, mobile phones.	Bridge construction, building a hospital.	Confectionery (chocolates), medicine.
Features	Job cost records prepared with all relevant costs.	As job costing, but the price per unit is found by dividing total batch costs by the number of units produced.	Contract accounts kept for each contract. Progress payments depend on work certified. Profits can be taken before contract completed, but losses must also be recognised.	Costs of one process added to those of subsequent processes until total cost found. Unit cost found by dividing total production cost by number of units produced in a specific period.

Question 10 ....

Does your organisation, or one with which you are familiar, use any form of activity based management?

Whether it does or not, what do you think would be the potential benefits to this particular organisation of such techniques?

You may find it helpful to read the article by Rutherford (2001) 'ABC: too much activity and not enough costing?' in ACCA's *Accounting & Business*. This can be downloaded from the B292 website.

References

Brimson, J. and Fraser, R. (1991) 'The key features of ABB', *Management Accounting*, vol. 69, no. 1, p. 42–3.

CIMA Official Terminology (2005), Oxford, CIMA Publishing.

Guilding, G. and McManus, L. (2002) 'The incidence, perceived merit and antecedents of customer accounting: an exploratory note', *Accounting, Organizations and Society*, vol. 27, no. 1–2, pp. 45–59.

Johnson, S. (2004) 'Just-in-time operations and backflush accounting', ACCA Accounting & Business [online] www.accaglobal.com/students/student_accountant/archive/2004/46/1143053 (accessed 27 April 2010).

McLaney, E. and Atrill P. (2008) *Accounting: An Introduction* (4th edn), Pearson Education, Harlow, UK.

McWatters, C.S., Zimmerman, J.L. and Morse, D.C. (2008) *Management Accounting: Analysis and Interpretation*, Pearson Education, Harlow, UK.

Raturi, A.S. and Singhal, V.R. (1990) 'Estimating the opportunity cost of capital for inventory investments', *OMEGA: The International Journal of Management Science*, vol. 18, no. 4, pp. 407–13.

Rutherford, B. (2001) 'ABC: too much activity and not enough costing?', ACCA Accounting & Business [online], www.accaglobal.com/students/dipfm/finance_matters/archive/2001/46/15723 (accessed 3 February 2010).

Weetman P. (2006) *Financial and Management Accounting: An Introduction* (4th edn), Pearson Education, Harlow, UK.

Acknowledgements

Grateful acknowledgement is made to the following sources.

Cover image: iStockphoto.com

Text

Page 70: Johnson, S. (2004) Just-in-time operations and backflush accounting, www.accaglobal.com, 27 April.

Page 75: Rutherford, B. (2001) ABC: too much activity and not enough costing? www.accaglobal.com, 3 February.

Figures

Figure 10. Brimson, J. and Fraser, R. (1991) 'The key features of ABB', *Management Accounting*, January, Volume 69, No. 1. The British Library.

Illustrations

Page 9: Rex Baloo © www.CartoonStock.com

Page 15: Andrew Toos © www.CartoonStock.com

Page 24: Mike Flanagan © www.CartoonStock.com

Page 45: Rex Baloo © www.CartoonStock.com

Page 50: Classic Mini Cooper © iStockphoto.com, Luca Morreale.

Every effort has been made to contact copyright holders. If any have been inadvertently overlooked the publishers will be pleased to make the necessary arrangements at the first opportunity.